W9-ANB-502

The Therapeutic "Aha!"

A NORTON PROFESSIONAL BOOK

THE THERAPEUTIC "AHA!"

10 Strategies for Getting Your Clients Unstuck

COURTNEY ARMSTRONG

W. W. NORTON
New York • London

Printed in the United States of America
First Edition

For information about permission to reproduce selections from this book,
write to Permissions, W. W. Norton & Company, Inc.,
500 Fifth Avenue, New York, NY 10110

For information about special discounts for bulk purchases, please contact
W. W. Norton Special Sales at specialsales@wwnorton.com or 800-233-4830

Manufacturing by Maple Press
Production manager: Christine Critelli

978-0-393-70840-0

W. W. Norton & Company, Inc.
500 Fifth Avenue, New York, N.Y. 10110
www.wwnorton.com

W. W. Norton & Company Ltd.
Castle House, 75/76 Wells Street, London W1T 3QT

1 2 3 4 5 6 7 8 9 0

To Joel and Buzz
who loved and tamed my emotional brain.

Contents

PART III: ACTIVATING EXPERIENTIAL CHANGE

Acknowledgments

Thanks to the wonderful team at W. W. Norton, especially to my editor Andrea Costella Dawson who initiated this project and Ben Yarling and Katie Moyer for seeing it through to completion. I also want to thank Leslie Anglin for her sharp editing eye and enthusiasm. Of course, this book would not have been possible if it weren't for my mentors Jon Connelly and Bill O'Hanlon and I am so grateful for their creativity, wisdom, and encouragement. Thanks also to Rich Simon for helping me find my writer's voice, Penny Randolph for her lovely illustration, and to Tyler Orr for his modeling and support. My gratitude also goes out to Sam Gershman, Jaak Panksepp, Joe LeDoux, Seymour Epstein, Lori Katz, Bruce Ecker, and Simon d'Orsogna for taking the time to answer questions and process my thoughts as I worked out applications of scientific research into practical therapeutic strategies. I must also thank my good friends and colleagues Tara Dickherber, Jean Griffis, Nancy Gershman, and Vicky Baltz for their ongoing support and encouragement through this project. Finally, my heartfelt appreciation goes out to my clients who have taught me the most about healing, the therapeutic relationship, and the amazing resilience of the human spirit. For all of you, I am grateful.

The Therapeutic "Aha!"

Introduction: The Power of Emotion

Watching a client transform from a state of angst to enlightenment is exhilarating for a psychotherapist. Even more thrilling is the rare "Aha!" moment, when a certain realization clicks into place, releases the client from the shackles of an imprisoning belief, and liberates the client toward change. We have all had those eureka experiences in our sessions, but why do they seem so elusive? Do people really make lasting change after they have had such epiphanies? More important, what can you do when the therapy process seems stuck and absolutely no flashes of insight are coming? Is there a certain set of conditions that seem to facilitate therapeutic breakthroughs in sessions? I believe that there is. It all starts with understanding the power of emotion and how to use it in a way that promotes positive shifts in both mind and brain.

Since the dawn of time, humans have attempted to tame passion with reason, usually with limited success. Plato (trans. 2005) compared balancing emotion and reason to a small charioteer attempting to steer two horses running in opposite directions. Centuries later, albeit during the Age of Reason, philosophers such as David Hume concluded, "Reason is, and ought only to be the slave of the passions, and can never pretend to any other office than to serve and obey them" (1738/2011, p. 174). Even modern neuroscientists acknowledge the futility of attempting to control emotions with rationality, as neuroscientist Joe LeDoux sings with his band, The Amygdaloids (2007): "An emotional brain is a hard thing to tame/It just won't stay in its place/Every time I think I got it /It gives me another face."[1]

[1] used with permission of Joseph LeDoux.

LeDoux's lyrics in this song refer to the fact that our brains are biologically structured so that when our emotional systems are strongly aroused, they have the capacity to easily override our rational, cognitive systems. We don't need a brain scan to validate this phenomenon. We know it through our experience living as human beings. How many times have you surprised yourself by jumping at the scary part of a movie or shouting something hurtful at someone you love when you feel angry? Although you know the villain in the movie isn't real and the insult to your loved one will only make things worse, your emotional brain ignores this logic and leaps into action. In essence, the emotional brain *is* our unconscious mind, and scientists estimate that it controls, or at least influences, about 95% of what we do, think, and feel at any given moment.

THE EMOTIONAL BRAIN

Sitting deep in the midbrain between the cortex and brain stem, the emotional brain, or mammalian brain, as pioneering neuroscientist Paul MacLean (1990) called it, is where the majority of neural networks for our attachment schemas, implicit memories, and automatic patterns are stored. Most of the patterns stored in the emotional brain are learned experientially and activated unconsciously.

Contrary to what Freud theorized, the emotional brain is not merely driven by shadowy sexual urges or simplistic self-gratification, nor does it harbor "repressed" feelings. While it is true that the emotional brain drives our instincts for survival and pleasure, this "lower brain" isn't as self-serving as we've been led to believe. In fact, as you will learn in Chapter 1, this area of the brain also prompts us to be interested in connecting with others, giving and receiving care, pursuing playful activities, and seeking experiences that inspire us and add to the quality of our lives. After all, life without emotion would be quite dull and seem rather meaningless.

While the emotional brain is generally adaptive and well intentioned, it isn't really fazed by quiet, rational discussion, intellectual insight, or analytical arguments—some of the staples of modern psychotherapy. Instead, the emotional brain learns from experience, association, stimulation of the senses, and repetition. Therefore, no matter how brilliantly our prefrontal cortex delivers intellectual insight and plans elegant coping strategies, the emotional brain is primed to override it all with neural patterns that persist until we intervene with something our emotional brain can understand: *a compelling felt experience.*

Orchestrating such felt experiences goes beyond simple emotional awareness or emotional catharsis around the problem. Therapists must elicit an affectively engaging experience that changes the *emotional meaning* of an event. Hitting this neural sweet spot where cognition and emotion synthesize is what I believe creates that "Aha" moment.

Cognitive-experiential theorist Seymour Epstein (2014) might call this a *cognitive-experiential* form of therapy because the therapist is still aiding the client in identifying unhelpful thoughts and beliefs but assists the client in changing negative beliefs through the brain's subcortical experiential learning systems. Acknowledging the necessity of engaging both rational and experiential systems is especially relevant for intellectual clients who understand their problems all too well but have not been able to change in spite of their insight, like my client Saundra.

SAUNDRA'S SUNRISE

Saundra was an attractive, talented surgeon with a Mensa-level IQ who graduated at the top of her class from an Ivy League school. She struggled most of her life with waves of severe depression and anxiety, but in recent years her mood swings had become more frequent and stormy, flooding her personal life and threatening to wreck her career. When she arrived at my office, Saundra clenched her jaw and gripped her wrist as she expressed feeling extremely disappointed with herself. "Intellectually," she lamented, "I understand what causes the depression and anxiety. Trust me, I've had years of therapy and tried dozens of medications. I realize my thoughts are irrational and know I developed these patterns because my family of origin was critical, abusive, and chaotic. But I'm 40 years old. When am I going to get over it?"

As Saundra described her history, I realized she had an excellent grasp of her issues and did not need more knowledge about her situation, nor did she need assistance recognizing cognitive distortions. She saw them staring back at her in bold, living color and put lots of energy into reframing them. Yet her attempts to reason her way out of her feelings only added to her frustration and feelings of inadequacy. It occurred to me that what Saundra was really seeking was a new experience of herself. An experience that would cause her to believe there was more to her than negativity. As we talked, I began to search for experiences or subjects that elicited a smile on her face, passion in her voice, or animated movement in her body. What in Saundra's life makes it worth coming to see me? What topics seemed to relax her or energize her?

Watching and listening for these cues, it became clear to me that the dearest things to Saundra's heart were her children. Describing her children was the only thing that seemed to brighten her eyes and broaden her affect into a slight smile. In addition, the rigidity in Saundra's posture softened whenever she talked about painting or being outside in nature. Since she enjoyed painting, I assumed she was good at visualizing things, so I asked Saundra to recall a place in nature where she saw something that was beautiful and awe inspiring. She described watching the sunrise by a cool, calm lake in a wooded area near her home. As she described this scene to me, she released a deep sigh, closed her eyes, and leaned back into the curve of the couch. Her jaw relaxed and her clenched fingers unfolded as she rested her hands on her lap. She took another deep breath and whispered, "I could linger there for hours."

Because she was beginning to relax and indicated an interest in going further, I narrated the scene back to her, adjusting the pitch and tone of my voice so that it was melodic, soothing, and uplifting. I colorfully elaborated on the description of her sunrise, suggesting she could enjoy noticing how the crimson edges melted into pleasant pinks and golden oranges that glowed against the backdrop of a serene azure sky and the cool, calm lake. She dropped her tense shoulders as I continued using sensory-rich language to describe the balmy feel of the air and the fresh pine scent of the trees, and made soft sound effects of the wind and birdsong. Like an enchanting storyteller, narrating guided imagery with sound effects, animation in your voice, and sensory descriptive words is a great way to make an experience come alive for the emotional brain.

When I asked Saundra what she was noticing within herself, Saundra sighed as she murmured, "Feelings of serenity, peace and joy." I suggested to her that I did not think the sunrise dropped those feelings of peace inside of her. Instead, I told her I thought she was getting in touch with her true nature, who she really was underneath the clouds of depression. I added, "Just like the sun is not destroyed by dark clouds and rainy days, we know your light is not destroyed because you just got in touch with it when you were imagining that scene." Tears streamed down her face as Saundra nodded and placed her hand over her heart, stating, "That is the sweetest thing I have ever heard. I do think that is who I am under all this darkness, but if I showed this side of myself to anyone, it got squelched. I am careful not to squelch my kids. I want them to feel free to express themselves and not feel so afraid, like I felt as a kid."

Utilizing her passion for being a loving, supportive parent informed our work in subsequent sessions as we used other types of imagery in which Saundra envisioned stepping into traumatic scenes from her youth and reparented her younger self with the same nurturing, guiding, protective responses she gave to her children. Within 2 months, Saundra developed a new relationship with herself and her emotions. She reported fewer mood swings and was handling interpersonal situations more effectively. Rather than engaging in endless thought loops of self-talk when she felt discouraged, Saundra imagined her sunrise and sent herself feelings of love and reassurance to calm down. She was less fearful of getting "squelched" if she showed her soft side to others. Saundra commented, "Other therapists told me I needed to learn to love myself, but nobody ever *showed* me how to do that." Saundra was right. She could have never *thought* her way into loving herself. She needed someone who could lead her and show her how to *evoke* the experience of self-compassion.

THE ART OF EVOKING EMOTION

Showing up for my clients in this more creative, provocative way was not an easy transition for me. I was trained traditionally in cognitive-behavioral therapy and was very good at delivering it with the kind of empathy that would rival Carl Rogers. My practice was busy and my clients liked me, but to be honest, I rarely witnessed those crystallizing breakthrough moments. People would gain insight and try out the skills I suggested. They would feel better for a time, but the changes would not stick unless we met for months and the client put a lot of effort into consciously applying the skills between sessions.

That all changed several years ago when I stumbled upon a hypnosis workshop taught by an unconventional, but brilliant therapist named Jon Connelly (2014), who calls his method Rapid Resolution Therapy™. I heard his method was especially effective for clearing the negative impact of trauma. On his Web site, I watched an impressive demonstration video of his work with a 9-11 World Trade Center bombing survivor that made me want to learn more. When I attended my first training session in Orlando, I expected to learn about new scientific breakthroughs and to pick up a few innovative techniques. What I was not expecting was essentially a theatrical performance led by this spellbinding 1960s peace activist turned therapist who showed up as fusion of artist, actor, stand-up comedian, and evangelical-like healer. He is the one who taught me the concepts I used in the imagery exercise with Saundra. Connelly's use of poetic words and dramatic performance art in his trainings, *and* with his clients, convinced me it's less about the intervention and more about how we use ourselves in the session to create a therapeutic experience. He taught me not to get overly focused on why the client developed the problem but instead to ask myself, "What is my intention for this client? What effect do I want our conversation to have on this person?"

Then it dawned on me. I learned a similar concept during my internship in graduate school 20 years ago when I worked with groups of at-risk students in New Orleans. The traditional cognitive-behavioral interventions I tried didn't faze those kids at all. I realized I'd better come up with a more entertaining song and dance routine fast—or those kids would fry up my self-esteem in no time and serve it back to me in a gumbo steeped in red-hot humiliation. So I left my textbooks by the Mississippi River and brought in art supplies and music as we spent time writing raps, telling stories, improvising skits, and honestly discussing our backgrounds and cultures. The magic started happening when I stopped hiding behind a detached therapist persona and began connecting with these students emotionally, crafting experiences that helped them face their fears and move closer to what they really wanted—feeling a sense of worth, purpose, and connection to something larger than themselves.

We spontaneously came up with ideas like developing a mock shoe design business, which led the students to learn how to work more cooperatively with others, believe they could have a future outside the ghetto, and see that an education could actually get them somewhere. I dared them to be more emotionally open by telling them I would reward them with an "awkward white-girl dance" any time they dropped the tough gangbanger facade and admitted to feeling scared or sad. They loved that. It was a funny, experiential way to reduce the threat of expressing their feelings to the group members while simultaneously teaching them that emotional vulnerability was universal.

EMOTIONAL PARADIGM SHIFT

After my stint in the New Orleans School system, I worked at hospitals and doctors' offices and eventually opened a private practice. While my time in the medical field was valuable, I realized I'd gotten so caught up in following the medical model and keeping up with managed care requirements that I'd lost the spontaneity that fueled the early years of my career. Connelly's work reminded me to listen to my clinical intuition, develop my own creative style, and be more emotionally engaging with clients. As I incorporated these qualities and a few of the methods I learned from him, I began having breakthrough sessions almost immediately. Hungry for a deeper understanding of why this approach was working so well,

I began to devour books and research on trauma, positive psychology, experiential modalities, and affective neuroscience.

Fortunately, I learned that brain science seems to be validating what we have intuitively known as therapists: People heal through meaningful emotional experiences with others. In addition to Connelly's Rapid Resolution Therapy model, most of the newer psychotherapy models emphasize experiential-emotional integration and have research to back up their effectiveness, including emotion-focused therapy, interpersonal neurobiology, eye movement desensitization and reprocessing, somatic experiencing, coherence therapy, accelerated experiential dynamic psychotherapy, Hakomi, sensorimotor therapy, and holographic reprocessing.

To start, all these approaches highlight the healing power of creating emotional attunement with the client. As Dan Siegel (2010a) describes it, emotional attunement gives the client the sense of "feeling felt," and it is one of the hallmarks of secure attachment. Study after study shows it's the therapeutic relationship that promotes change more than any single technique. But what kind of relationship promotes change? I've learned that simply mirroring and validating clients' experience is not enough; we also have to know how to artfully lift and lead clients so that they feel motivated and believe they can reach their goals. The chapters in Part I: Awakening a Session show you how to connect with your clients in not just a caring way but also a compelling way that inspires them and triggers their desire to take action.

In addition to creating an emotionally responsive relationship with clients, you have to identify and reprocess implicit memories retained from traumatic experiences that frequently drive unwanted patterns and beliefs. Simply encouraging clients to get in touch with painful emotions and vent them through experiential reenactment techniques is counterproductive. Not only are such reenactment approaches painful and inefficient, but they can also reinforce unwanted patterns and retraumatize clients. Similarly, cognitive-behavioral therapy addresses conscious manifestations of trauma and learned patterns, but it often involves excruciating exposure techniques and doesn't always reach the nonverbal, implicit meanings that were formed during a traumatic encounter.

The insufficiency of these "top-down approaches" has led to newer psychotherapy models, such as Pat Ogden's sensorimotor psychotherapy (Ogden & Minton, 2006) and Peter Levine's somatic experiencing (1997), which treat trauma by encouraging a "bottom-up" processing of nonverbal, somatic aspects of memory. But what if you could update an implicit pattern in a nonpainful way at its source so that it couldn't even turn on anymore? Recent neuroscience discoveries regarding the process of memory reconsolidation suggest that there is a way to reconstruct memories in a less painful way; however, there appears to be a specific process that must be followed for the emotional brain to unlock and update these memories. We will detail the findings on memory reconsolidation and a specific protocol you can use in Part II: Healing Emotional Wounds. Additionally, I will show you how to adapt this reconsolidation process into your current approach so that you don't have to learn a whole new model of therapy.

In Part III: Activating Experiential Change, you will learn a number of experiential strategies that recruit positive emotional systems, like care and play, to resolve problems. In fact, researchers who have studied "Aha!" moments found that a positive mood biases our cognitive systems in ways that facilitate insight (Kounios & Beeman, 2009; Subramaniam, Kounios, Parrish, & Jung-Beeman, 2009). For example, storytelling is one of the best ways to lighten the mood and facilitate learning through both the rational and emotional parts of the brain. So I'll be weaving in stories and client examples to give you a feel for how to implement the strategies in this book. You can also watch video examples on my website at http://www.courtneyarmstrong.net.

You don't have to be a brain scientist to realize that appealing to people's emotions is the fastest way to propel change; but for those of you who want to understand the brain science that supports these techniques, the next chapter will provide the basic mechanics of the emotional brain. For those who would rather dive straight into the 10 strategies, you can skip to Chapter 2, Enlivening the Therapeutic Alliance.

PART I

AWAKENING A SESSION

CHAPTER 1

Engaging the Emotional Brain

Recent neuroscience discoveries have validated what Freud suspected all along: Something beneath the hood of our skulls is running the show in spite of our rational, conscious intentions. Meet your emotional brain, also the area that Yale neuroscientist and triune brain theorist Paul MacLean (1990) referred to as the "mammalian" brain because all mammals, including humans, have this part of the brain. The emotional brain is home to our affective response systems, and it is also where the bulk of our networks for emotional memories, attachment schemas, and automatic behavior patterns are stored. Freud referred to this area as the "unconscious," and we could still think of this deeper part of the brain as "unconscious" because we are not fully conscious of how it generates an emotional response or influences our behaviors. Instead, we are only consciously aware of the outcome, whether we experience that outcome as a strong emotion, a "gut" feeling, or an urge to do something.

USER-FRIENDLY GUIDE TO THE EMOTIONAL BRAIN

You certainly don't have to be a neuroscientist to be an effective therapist, but I would like to provide an overview of the basic mechanisms involved in emotional processing so you can better understand the rationale behind the interventions that I present in this book.

As MacLean (1990) described in his theory of the triune brain, the brain could be divided into three areas somewhat layered on top of the other: (1) the reptilian brain, (2) the mammalian brain, and (3) the cerebral cortex. Although MacLean's concept of the triune brain is now thought to be too simplistic for describing complex brain anatomy, it can still serve as a useful model for understanding the "bottom-up" architecture of the brain from a psychotherapy standpoint. So I'll start with this concept and then transition to the more modern view of multiple emotional systems that connect all areas of the brain. In the following sections I've referenced the major brain regions that I think are of primary interest to psychotherapists. This is not meant to be an extensive, detailed description of all brain regions, but just enough to give you a rudimentary understanding. Figure 1.1 provides an illustration you can reference as you read about the following parts of the brain.

Brain Stem and Basal Ganglia (Reptilian Brain)

The brain stem and basal ganglia make up what MacLean (1990) referred to as the reptilian brain. The brain stem regulates our most basic bodily functions such as heart rate, body temperature, breathing, blood pressure, and reflexes that we are born knowing how to do, such as grasping and sucking.

The basal ganglia are a collection of structures located within the temporal lobes on both sides of the thalamus. The basal ganglia play an important role in planning and coordinating voluntary motor movements and posture. Procedural learning related to routine behaviors, habits, and addiction is also associated with this brain region because the nucleus accumbens, the reward center of the brain, is included in the basal ganglia.

Emotional Brain/Limbic Areas (Mammalian Brain)

The emotional brain lies in the midbrain between the brain stem and cerebral cortex. In addition to being the seat of our emotional responses, like the fight-flight-or-freeze response, this area of the brain is involved in procedural learning, motivation, and memory. MacLean (1990) referred to the emotional area of the brain as the *mammalian* brain because all mammals, including humans, share these regions that are primarily concerned with preserving and promoting the survival of one's species. MacLean also coined the term "limbic system" as a way to refer to the midbrain areas that are involved in generating emotional responses. Even though there is disagreement among neuroscientists as to which structures should be included in the limbic system, I will focus on the five main structures that are of most interest to psychotherapists.

- *Thalamus.* The thalamus sits at the top of the brain stem and receives all sensory input; it determines whether the information will be kept in temporary awareness or passed through to higher levels of the brain and long-term memory storage.
- *Hypothalamus.* The hypothalamus sits under the thalamus. Although it is a small structure about the size of a peanut, it controls our autonomic nervous system and regulates body temperature, sleep/wake cycles, food intake, and thirst.
- *Amygdala.* The amygdala is involved in emotional learning and is most known for its role in processing and activating the emotion of fear. The amygdala was named after the Greek word for "almond" because it is an almond-shaped structure located within the temporal lobe on each side of the brain that is fully developed by the eighth month of gestation. The amygdala receives sensory information from the thalamus, assesses the emotional value of a stimulus based on past learning, and prompts the nervous system to approach or avoid something based on this appraisal. Because the amygdala has direct neural connections to the hypothalamus, motor cortex circuits, and brain stem, it can activate a rapid survival response before we consciously realize what spooked us.

  The amygdala is also involved in attachment, processing facial expressions and other social signals of emotion. It encodes the somatic markers of our emotional experiences in a nonverbal, implicit, "felt" form and can generalize emotional associations to any stimulus that seems similar. Phobias, post-traumatic stress, projection, and transference are examples of unconscious appraisals involving the amygdala.

- *Hippocampus.* The hippocampus is shaped like a seahorse and sits directly behind the amygdala on each side of the brain. The hippocampus organizes experiences into time, context, and space and is associated with explicit, conscious forms of memory and learning. While the amygdala generalizes the meaning of a stimulus, the hippocampus helps to differentiate the nuances. For example, the amygdala could cause you to jump when you see a long, dark, curvy object lying in the grass beside your foot, but the hippocampus reminds you that the object is too still to be a snake and is, in fact, only a fallen tree limb.

The hippocampus does not fully come online until we are about 3 or 4 years old, and it continues to develop into our adulthood. Therefore, our earliest memories are primarily processed through nonverbal, implicit, amygdaloid memory systems. Likewise, when we experience an event that is emotionally overwhelming or traumatic, the neurochemistry associated with strong emotional arousal inhibits hippocampal processing while quickly imprinting the sensory data of the experience into implicit memory systems.

For this reason, we can be haunted by the experience of a disturbing event without being able to put it into words, context, or a coherent narrative. Sometimes we are not even aware of the actual event that caused the emotional reaction we are having. We just know we feel overcome with emotions that seem out of proportion to the present situation, yet we cannot stop the emotions or reason them away.

- *Insular cortex.* The insula receives information from receptors in the skin and the body's internal organs to produce subjective feeling states. It is through the insula that we acquire our interoceptive state of awareness and sense what others may be feeling. In addition, this small area on either side of the brain generates emotions thought to be uniquely human, such as pride, guilt, disgust, and our appreciation for the emotional component of music and art. The insula relays information about these subjective feeling states to the anterior cingulate cortex and prefrontal cortex (discussed later) and provides emotional input that influences our decision making (Damasio, 2010).

Cerebral Cortex (Neocortex)

The cerebral cortex is the top, outer layer of the brain that is involved in our higher thinking and reasoning functions. The cerebral cortex governs our ability to speak and understand language and organizes our conscious perceptions of the world and ourselves.

- *Anterior cingulate cortex* (ACC). The ACC is in a unique position because its ventral (belly) area surrounds the limbic areas that we discussed earlier, while its dorsal (back) area connects with the prefrontal cortex, which we will discuss later. Because this region can receive signals from both regions, it can be viewed as a kind of bridge between attention and emotion functions, integrating cognition and affect. This area is involved in regulating emotions and pain, and it contributes to our conscious response to unpleasant experiences.
- *Prefrontal cortex (PFC).* In the foremost area of the cerebral cortex, sitting behind the eye sockets and forehead, is the PFC. The PFC is more highly developed in humans than it is in other species and is the area of the brain where we do most of our conscious, analytical thinking. Many therapeutic interventions, such as cognitive therapy, appeal to the prefrontal cortex's ability to assess situations logically, evaluate evidence, and plan coping strategies. According to researchers such as Pessoa (2013), areas of the ventromedial PFC and

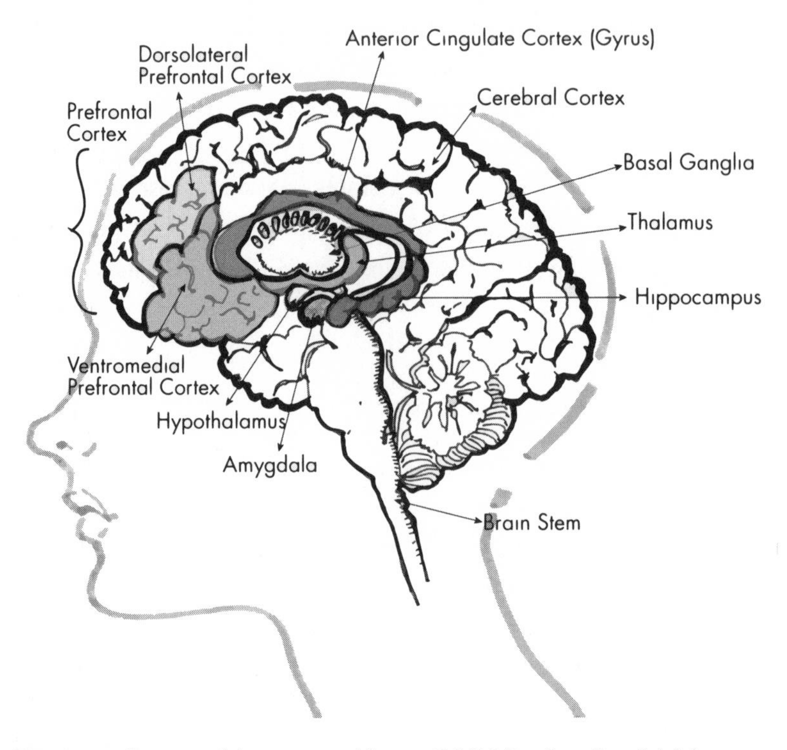

Figure 1.1 Regions of the emotional brain. © 2014 Penelope Randolph/ Randolph Design Group.

dorsolateral PFC are able to integrate input from both our rational and emotional systems. However, emotional and reasoning processes compete for resources in these areas of the brain. When emotional arousal is low, the executive and emotional areas of the brain can share this space quite nicely, producing great insights and wisdom. Yet, when emotional arousal is high, massive connections that shoot up from various structures in the emotional brain are capable of dominating these areas of the PFC. This is why you may be able to intellectually understand why you do what you do, yet have difficulty overriding a strong automatic response with simple reasoning and self-talk.

ALL EMOTION IS A REQUEST FOR AN ACTION

When you experience an emotion, it is not because your mind wants you to feel bad; it is simply your mind's way of getting you to do something that it believes would be in the best interest of your survival or the survival of your loved ones. In essence, all emotion is a request for an action. As biologist Robert Sapolsky (1994) discussed in his book *Why Zebras Don't Get Ulcers*, this stress response is only meant to last a few minutes, just long enough to take a useful action that promotes survival. Unfortunately, the emotional brain has difficulty distinguishing between what's imagined and what's real, so humans can activate an emotional response with a brief recollection of a past memory or the mere thought of possible future events.

Because the emotional brain has so many direct connections to our bodily systems, it instantly mobilizes energy in the form of hormones, glucose, and oxygen and compels us to respond to its request regardless of whether our rational mind thinks it's a good idea. For example, the emotion of fear is simply a request to move away from something the emotional brain deems dangerous, while the emotion of excitement is a request to move toward something that seems pleasurable. But it makes no difference to your emotional brain whether the feared stimulus is a grizzly bear or an angry boss; the physiological response is the same because both stimuli are perceived as threats.

The emotional systems involved in generating fear responses have been of great interest to therapists treating posttraumatic stress, phobias, and other anxiety disorders. Joe LeDoux, author of *The Emotional Brain* (1996) and a professor of neuroscience at New York University, was one of the first researchers to explore how the brain processes the emotional meaning of stimuli, particularly how the brain registers fear. LeDoux found that when a strong emotional response is coupled with an experience, the pattern is learned quickly without much repetition because the emotional brain releases hormones and modulatory neurochemicals that sear a behavioral response pattern in like glue.

Many a therapist has witnessed this when a client can still be completely overcome with fear in the face of a certain sensory trigger, in spite of his or her awareness that the trigger is actually harmless. An example would be the war veteran who runs for cover when he hears a loud bang outside on New Year's Eve. In spite of his awareness that the noise was most likely a firecracker, systems in the emotional brain have been conditioned to mobilize him to safety as quickly as possible. When the emotional brain is strongly aroused in this way, scientists estimate that it is controlling about 95% of what we feel, think, or do; however, our neocortex—what we might think of as the rational, intellectual mind—is only controlling about 5% (Zaltman, 2003). When you are in a life-or-death situation, having the emotional brain take over is a useful, efficient function.

For example, imagine you're driving home from work and talking on the phone to your friend Sally, when suddenly an oncoming car veers into your lane. In this case it's adaptive to follow your emotional brain's impulse to throw the cell phone down and swerve out of the way. One second of analytical deliberation by your prefrontal cortex could cost your life. Not realizing what happened, Sally may have thought your hanging up on her suddenly was very rude. But, when you later explain what happened, she'll probably understand and express gratitude that you didn't have an accident.

Unfortunately, because the emotional brain has trouble distinguishing between an imagined threat and actual danger, it can also prompt us to react in ways that are not in our best interest. For example, on another day you and Sally are shopping for jeans at a new designer store. After Sally's third joke about the size of your derriere and the salesperson's attempt to steer you to the "Plus" section, you storm out of the store, shouting to Sally and the salesperson that they can stick their designer denim straight up their snobby noses! This emotional outburst proves a little harder for you and Sally to reconcile. Now both of your emotional brains are tagging each other as potential threats and prompting you to avoid one another. Even if you consciously understand that Sally's teasing just triggered old feelings of anger you had toward a critical parent, your emotional brain confuses similar and same, labeling Sally as a threat. No matter how much self-talk you do when you're around her, the same old resentful feelings can simmer beneath the surface. What's required is an experiential intervention that recruits positive emotional systems to heal the old wound with your parent, or at least foster more favorable associations with Sally. We'll get into these interventions later in the book.

A COGNITIVE-EXPERIENTIAL APPROACH TO CHANGE

Although the emotional brain is generally well intentioned, it has different priorities and speaks a very different language from the neocortex, which is more word and logic oriented. As we discussed earlier, the emotional brain learns through experience, association, stimulation of the senses, and repetition. Thus, if you want to change a pattern stored at the level of the emotional brain—like a recurring traumatic memory, habitual behavior, or attachment schema—then you have to speak the nonverbal, sensory, experiential language the emotional brain understands.

Seymour Epstein, a psychology professor at the University of Massachusetts–Amherst, proposed over 40 years ago that humans have two separate systems for processing information: analytical-rational and experiential-intuitive. Since the 1970s, Epstein has gathered a plethora of research to develop and support his cognitive-experiential theory and eloquently details it in his most recent book, *Cognitive-Experiential Theory: An Integrative Theory of Personality* (2014).

According to Epstein, humans have a rational system that operates via logical analysis, evaluation of factual evidence, and verbal processing. In my thinking, the neural correlate of the rational system is the neocortex area of the brain, particularly the prefrontal cortex and verbal regions. In addition to the rational system, humans also process information through experiential systems, like animals do. The experiential system learns through association and is conditioned through both external reward and punishment from the environment, as well as internal positive and negative affect generated by the emotional brain. For humans, emotional learning differs from simple behavioral learning in that our behavior and personalities are not just shaped by reward and punishment, but by the implicit *meanings* our minds attach to an experience.

Several other prominent researchers have proposed similar dual-processing models, including Daniel Kahneman, Nobel Prize–winning psychologist and author of *Thinking Fast and Slow* (2011); Evans (2008); Strack and Duetsch (2004); and even the father of cognitive therapy, Aaron Beck (1971). Meanwhile, researchers like Pessoa (2013) and Keren and Schul (2009) argue that the dual-system model is too simplistic and that the brain probably has *more* than two ways of processing information. In spite of this criticism, Epstein's cognitive-experiential theory (CET) is one of the most robust theories of human behavior and personality to date. CET avoids suggesting the rational and experiential systems are entirely separate and acknowledges individuals have preferences for the degree to which they process information rationally or experientially, depending on the person's temperaments, basic needs, and the circumstances of a situation. CET is also in line with modern integrative models of psychotherapy and essentially synthesizes the best of what psychoanalytic, cognitive-behavioral, social-learning, and phenomenological theories have to offer.

For example, cognitive therapy recognizes emotions, thoughts, and behavior are colored by the appraisals a person attaches to events, but CET recognizes those appraisals are often generated unconsciously and encoded in a nonverbal form in the experiential system (or emotional brain regions). Beck called these "automatic thoughts" and sought to bring these appraisals to the client's conscious awareness to promote change. Yet, because the experiential system is largely nonconscious and nonverbal, it is very difficult to change a learned pattern through conscious, verbal reasoning alone. Epstein (2014) explains:

> According to CET, an experientially acquired belief may not be changed at all when it is made conscious because it continues to operate according to the same rules and attributes of the experi-

> ential system as it did before . . . making an implicit experiential belief explicit is an important first step in correcting an experiential belief because once it is identified in the rational system, it can be treated experientially. (p. 235)

Epstein proposes that therapists continue to explore ways to engage the experiential system to effect deep, lasting change. You might argue that behavioral interventions are a form of experiential intervention and suggest that cognitive-behavioral therapy already addresses both systems. But I have found that facilitating change for problematic emotional patterns just by consciously implementing new behaviors takes a long time. Moreover, as we'll discuss in Chapters 4 and 5, if behavioral interventions are not timed correctly, the brain just creates two neural networks that compete for expression.

The key is to create conditions that facilitate an *experience* that changes the *implicit* meaning and purpose associated with an emotional pattern. Furthermore, when you add an element of novelty, intrigue, humor, or joy to the process of learning something new, the emotional brain really lights up and synthesizes new information in a deeper, more complete way (Willis, 2006).

In subsequent chapters of this book, you will become much more knowledgeable and skilled at understanding the secret language of the emotional brain, learn a number of interventions that positively engage emotional systems, and discover that you can treat a variety of clinical issues rather quickly with these cognitive-experiential strategies.

SEVEN PRIMARY EMOTIONAL SYSTEMS

We started the chapter by looking at the emotional brain through MacLean's triune brain model to give you a sense of how and why the emotional brain can override rational responses. Yet, as I stated earlier, the triune brain model is too simplistic because brain researchers have found that regions at each level of the brain serve multiple purposes and are involved in a number of brain operations. So rather than assigning specific regions to narrow limited functions, think of emotional processes as occurring in various networks that connect through regions in the brain stem, midbrain, and prefrontal cortex. Conceptualizing these affective states in terms of systems will not only help you understand the "emotional gear" in which the client is stuck, but it will also guide you in selecting appropriate interventions that can smoothly shift clients into a more balanced state—as you'll learn later in this book.

In their excellent book, *The Archaeology of Mind*, neuroscience researchers Jaak Panksepp and Lucy Biven (2012) distinguished seven primary emotional systems within the brain: (1) SEEKING/Desire, (2) FEAR/Anxiety, (3) RAGE/Anger, (4) LUST/Sex, (5) CARE/Nurturance, (6) PANIC/GRIEF/Distress, and (7) PLAY/Social Joy. While all of these systems interplay with one another, like the keys on a piano can play various chords, it is important to distinguish the emotional systems separately because each involves different brain networks and neurotransmitters. We really cannot lump findings about different emotions together. Distinguishing these systems may also cause us to better diagnose and treat mental disorders as we come to better understand how and why various emotional systems get out of balance.

SEEKING/Desire

When Panksepp described the various emotional systems in his writings, he capitalized the spelling to denote it as the name of a neural system, not simply an emotion. For the sake of clarity, I will do the same as I describe my understanding of the names and classifications of these systems. The first system Panksepp described is the SEEKING system. The neural networks involved in the SEEKING system are mostly fueled by the neurotransmitter dopamine and move us to action, giving us the impetus to "get up and go get it." The SEEKING system integrates with the other emotional systems in that it may prompt us to seek safety when the FEAR circuits are stimulated, or to seek a mate when our LUST circuits are ignited, or to seek CARE when our PANIC/GRIEF systems are alarmed. The SEEKING emotional system also appears to be involved with driving people to engage in compulsive repetitive behaviors, like substance abuse, obsessive cleaning, or playing slot machines because the reward they are SEEKING is either delivered in small, less than satisfying amounts or delivered intermittently.

Although behaviorists would describe this as operant conditioning, Panksepp and Biven believe conditioned behavior goes beyond simple reward and punishment. The authors cited a study in which hungry rats were trained to tap a lever to receive food but would only get the food in very small amounts at intermittent intervals. Not only did the rats compulsively press the lever, but they would also pace in the cage back and forth. After the animal exhausts its efforts to get the food "reward" from the area where the food is delivered, it paces back and forth because the SEEKING circuits are still on, compelling the animal to do something—anything, just take an action!

How many times do we see this play out when people compulsively return to painful relationships or engage in any number of other behaviors that they intellectually know won't satisfy them yet feel compelled to do anyway? It's because the SEEKING system is trying to get the person to do something to relieve pain, restore balance, or pursue something pleasurable.

FEAR/Anxiety

FEAR/Anxiety is the system with which most psychotherapists are familiar. Although it has been described as the fight-or-flight response, it is more accurate to describe it as the freeze-or-flight response because most mammals and humans freeze at the first sign of danger, and then flee. As cited earlier, LeDoux (2000, 2007) has done the most extensive research on the fear system, and his work has been instrumental in helping us understand how the brain learns a fear and processes the emotional meaning of stimuli. Most recently, LeDoux has been collaborating with colleagues to determine how the brain can unlearn a fear (Nader, Schafe, & LeDoux, 2000; Monfils, Cowansage, Klann, & LeDoux, 2009; Schiller et al., 2010). For years, neuroscientists were doubtful that a fear could ever be fully extinguished. Fortunately, recent discoveries regarding a process called memory reconsolidation demonstrate that the brain can unlearn a fear by retrieving a fear memory and following a specific process within a certain window of time upon recalling it to "erase" its emotional charge. This discovery has terrific implications for psychotherapy, particularly in the treatment of posttraumatic stress and anxiety disorders, but it is also being used to treat substance abuse. I'll go into more detail about the memory reconsolidation process and how to utilize it in your sessions in Chapter 5.

RAGE/Anger

The third emotional system that Panksepp distinguished is the RAGE/Anger system. Although the RAGE system closely parallels the FEAR system, there are subtle differences, biologically speaking. For example, the sections of the amygdala that are involved in activating rage responses are different from the sections that mediate fear. Similarly, the rage response travels a different pathway from the amygdala to the hypothalamus than the pathway that fear traverses through the brain.

RAGE circuits are triggered by restraint and frustration. In other words, RAGE erupts when the animal's attempt to SEEK what it wants is thwarted or threatened. Again, different emotional systems interplay with one another so the SEEKING and RAGE systems are often simultaneously engaged. RAGE and FEAR share many biological similarities involving the release of adrenaline and mobilization of glucose and oxygen to the limbs if we perceive a threat. Whether the RAGE or FEAR circuit gets activated depends on the meaning the amygdala attaches to the stimulus.

Ultimately, to eliminate feelings of RAGE or FEAR, the perception of a threat must be eliminated. Beating pillows or venting wildly about frustrations only seems to escalate RAGE because the SEEKING system has not been fully satisfied. Similarly, such behaviors will not necessarily extinguish anger or cause someone to feel more empowered either. In Parts II and III, we will discuss creative interventions that actually do eliminate the emotional brain's perception of a threat and relieve feelings of fear, anger, and rage quickly.

LUST/Sex

The fourth system that Panksepp distinguished is the LUST/Sexual system. In both males and females, the LUST system hooks up with the SEEKING system to activate the animal to pursue a mate and procreate. LUST systems are wired differently through the brain in males and females. For instance, male systems connect more through the visual circuits of the brain and mobilize neurochemicals that promote assertiveness. In contrast, female LUST systems connect through circuits that bind with oxytocin, a hormone that promotes bonding and interplays with the CARE emotional system that we'll discuss later in this chapter.

The discoveries about gender differences within our LUST systems validate why men and women are turned on by different stimuli and pursue mates differently. Men are decidedly more aroused with visual stimuli, while women are more aroused when they feel understood and cared about emotionally. That's not to say that women aren't turned on visually and men don't warm up when they feel cared about. This is just to note that men and women's sexual behaviors involve different circuitries that cause them to pursue sexual needs differently.

We didn't really need to wait for brain science to enlighten us to this fact. Poets, artists, and musicians have lyrically elaborated on the mysteries of lust and love since the beginning of time. In fact, if you want to improve your sex life, you are probably better off studying poetry and music, rather than neuroscience, but I'll save that topic for another book. For now, suffice it to say that you don't need to get bogged down in the mechanics of how the brain creates erotic experiences, but it is good to know enough to guide couples toward behavior that is more likely to lead to sexual and relationship satisfaction.

CARE/Nurturance

CARE/Nurturance is the fifth emotional system that Panksepp described. We now know that care and nurturing are not just nice to have if you can get them, but that our survival literally depends on them. Several animal studies and even human studies on orphans have demonstrated that infants who do not receive consistent care and nurturing fail to develop normally and even die prematurely. The clinical term for this unfortunate circumstance is called "failure to thrive." In fact, I have seen clients more severely impacted by childhood neglect than childhood abuse. Even my clients who experienced horrific abuse often say the feeling that nobody cared about them tormented them more than the actual violence they experienced. Similarly, clients who experienced neglect without any physical abuse seem just as emotionally conflicted as clients who were exposed to repeated violence. For these clients, feelings of guilt and shame are even more insidious because they cannot identify a concrete reason why they feel worthless and unwanted. Instead, they often make comments like "I cannot think of any particular trauma. My parents weren't outwardly mean to me, but I just felt like I wasn't really important to them."

The important thing for therapists to take away from the discovery of the CARE system is that we should not underestimate the power of developing a caring, therapeutic alliance with our clients. In Chapters 2 and 3, I will discuss several ways that you can develop a CARING alliance with your clients, while simultaneously prompting their SEEKING system to pursue what's in their best interest.

PANIC/GRIEF/Distress

The sixth emotional system is PANIC/GRIEF, which is best exemplified through the separation distress a baby duckling, or a baby human, feels when it is separated from its mother. Panksepp differentiated PANIC as involving slightly different systems than the FEAR system. From Panksepp's view, PANIC is more connected to the emotion of grief because it is what an animal experiences when it is separated from its mother, pack, or other loved ones. Although the PANIC/GRIEF system literally involves feelings of pain and terror, it is adaptive, biologically speaking. When a baby bird falls out of its nest and cries loudly, the cries of distress are intended to let the mother know where the baby bird is so she can find her little chick. Human mothers frequently report that they can distinguish their baby's cry from another child's cry when they are picking their child up at daycare or get separated from their child in a grocery store. The cries are to call the mother, the pack, or other loved ones back home. Even as adult humans we may feel the urge to moan and cry out in gut-wrenching pain when someone we love has died. It is the same separation-distress call baby animals make for their mothers.

Elephants instinctively understand that this separation-distress cry from another pachyderm is a request for comfort and CARE from the surviving members of the herd. Likewise, in many Eastern cultures and third-world countries, people think of grief occurring in community because there is an understanding that people need CARE and social connection during this time. Interestingly, I have found the root of panic disorder ultimately involves feeling separated from those we love or fearing social rejection on some level. Therefore, the antidote is to bring resolution to the original trauma that triggered feelings of intense separation distress and assist the client in developing a sense of safe connection with others. We'll discuss techniques for healing panic and grief distress in Chapters 6, 7, 9, and 10.

PLAY/Social Joy

The seventh emotional system that Panksepp delineated is the system of PLAY. Playfulness is actually hardwired into our brains and is a delightful way to connect with others, learn new skills, and cultivate joy in our lives. Play is also marvelously therapeutic; yet therapists avoid incorporating play and humor because they do not consider themselves creative, or they fear it would imply they are not taking the client's issues seriously. On the contrary, I have found that incorporating playfulness into one's sessions is a powerful way to strengthen the therapeutic alliance, relieve anxiety, extinguish anger, and teach clients a variety of new skills quickly. Throughout the book I will give you multiple examples of how to integrate playfulness into your therapeutic style, even if you think you are too low-key or reserved for that sort of thing.

In sum, although most therapists are familiar with the limbic system and its role in the fight-flight-or-freeze response, brain researchers have now identified seven distinct systems in the emotional brain that drive human responses and behavior. Awareness of these various systems can assist you in assessing where an emotional pattern is "stuck" and lends ideas for more effective, experiential interventions.

As Blaise Pascal stated in his book *Pensées*, "We know truth, not only by the reason, but also by the heart..." (1958, p. 80). That's what this book aims to do: to show you how to use the wisdom of emotion to reveal deeper truths within your clients, while wielding the energy of emotion to propel clients toward their goals. You begin by cultivating an affectively engaging connection with your client, which I'll discuss in the next chapter, Enlivening the Therapeutic Alliance.

CHAPTER 2

Enlivening the Therapeutic Alliance

Four decades of empirical research and over 1,100 studies confirm that it is the relationship between the therapist and client that is more impactful than any technique or therapeutic approach (Norcross, 2010). But exactly what kind of relationship promotes healing and change? I know it's not simply being a kind, empathic listener, like I was taught in graduate school. If that were true, then I ought to have clients, insurance companies, and family members eating out of the palm of my hand just by being attentive and nice.

In fact, if you observe any of the great therapists of our time, such as Carl Whitaker, Salvador Minuchin, or Virginia Satir, you'll see the one thing they have in common is the ability to establish a charismatic connection and evoke meaningful emotional experiences within their clients. You don't just want to have a compassionate conversation with your clients; you want to have an *influential* conversation that mobilizes them emotionally. Motivational speakers know how to stir people in this way and—dare I say?—so do many politicians and cult leaders. Yet the majority of modern therapists attempt to engage clients by enrolling them in a relatively quiet, intellectual conversation. This chapter will guide you in the art of enlivening the therapeutic alliance in a way that not only eases the client's pain but also spurs interest in change.

FOSTERING EARNED SECURE ATTACHMENT

Carl Rogers (1957) believed that creating the conditions of empathy, congruence, and nonjudgmental positive regard within the therapeutic relationship was sufficient for facilitating change. Similarly, a recent meta-analysis by Nissen-Lie, Monsen, and Ronnestad (2010) found these same three traits important; however, their research also revealed that clients preferred therapists who were *engaged and responsive.* In other words, clients want more than an empathic listener. They want a therapist who actively participates in the session, guiding and collaborating with them to do what's in their best interest.

That's not to say being a warm, empathic listener isn't a good place to start. Psychology researchers such as Dan Siegel (2010a), Allan Schore (2012), and Sue Johnson (2002) have compared the process of creating a strong therapeutic relationship to the process of creating secure attachment between parent and child. Parents set the stage for creating secure attachment with their infant by attuning to the baby's emotional states with a level of interest and empathy that causes the child to feel understood and cared for. UCLA researcher and therapist Allan Schore (2012) believes that when the caregiver models this understanding responsiveness to the child, it literally contributes to healthy development of areas within the brain associated with affect regulation and empathy.

Optimistically, Schore believes therapists can facilitate an "earned secured attachment" within the therapeutic relationship. You earn secure attachment by demonstrating empathy, interest, and emotional responsiveness as you tune into the client's nonverbal communication, not just the external content of what the client is saying.

GETTING IN YOUR RIGHT MIND

You are probably aware that the majority of our communication is transmitted nonverbally, but do you know how much? Dr. Albert Mehrabian, author of *Silent Messages* (1971), studied this extensively and estimated nonverbal communication makes up as much as 93% of conveying a message, whereas the words themselves contribute to only 7% of a message. Mehrabian noted that 55% of communication is expressed through body language like gestures, facial expressions, and posture, while 38% of communication is reflected through vocal elements such as voice tone, inflection, and prosody of speech.

Interpreting and transmitting nonverbal elements of communication are all specialties of the right hemisphere, which has more direct connections to the emotional brain than the left hemisphere. In fact, because verbal centers in the left hemisphere of the brain don't actually come online until we are around 2 years old, parents can only model connection and emotional regulation to their babies nonverbally. Consequently, the bulk of our early attachment schemas are represented in a felt, sensory way that is not readily explicit or conscious.

These implicit schemas form the foundation of how we connect with others as adults, so that most relational communication going on between people is occurring nonverbally, right brain to right brain. Your ability to mindfully tune into this implicit conversation transpiring between you and the client can provide you with a wealth of information. Although your left hemisphere will be tempted to interpret these paralinguistic cues in terms of transference and countertransference, my advice is to avoid intellectual interpretation. Instead, simply observe the nonverbal signals from the client as well as the intuitive impressions you sense in your own body in a curious, nonjudgmental way.

LOOKING BENEATH THE SURFACE

Most clients come to us because the rational part of their mind wants to make a change, but emotionally, they can't bring themselves to do it. These clients can't move forward until you bring this emotional conflict to the surface. For instance, a client I'll call Teresa smiled faintly and stated, "Courtney, my son has been sober for a few weeks now, but I can't stop the compulsive urge to check on him daily and make sure he hasn't relapsed. I realize that I need to back off and let my son take responsibility for his recovery. But, I can't stop ruminating about it. Can you just hypnotize me to let it go?"

Although Teresa was friendly and upbeat in her tone, as she spoke I felt a tight clench in my jaw and a disturbing tension in my stomach, like a volcano was brewing. I thought, "Is this my tension, or am I feeling Teresa's agitation?" Once I asked myself this question, I immediately got in touch with feelings of sadness and compassion. It was clear that I was not frustrated with Teresa; I was sensing *her* sadness and frustration. I knew that before Teresa could really let go, she had to work out the emotional conflict she had around detachment and give voice to her unexpressed feelings of anger and fear.

After pausing to check in with what I was sensing nonverbally, I invited Teresa to check in with her emotions. This is how the conversation unfolded:

Therapist: I admire your positive attitude and determination, Teresa. Yet part of the detachment process includes feelings that can seem scary or overwhelming like sadness, anger, or helplessness. Tune into your body for a moment and tell me if you sense any of those feelings as you release responsibility for your son's recovery.

Teresa: Yes. I feel angry.

Therapist: Mm-hmm and where do you feel that in your body?

Teresa: My jaw and my stomach. It's tight, like I'm holding something back.

Therapist: Okay, that makes sense. See if you can release a little of that tightness, like you're gently loosening a valve to discharge some steam.

Teresa: [Inhales, then lets out a big sigh as she loosens her jaw]

Therapist: Great. Do that again and as you exhale, give voice to what you've been holding back. There's no judgment here. I want to understand.

Teresa: Damn it, Bobby! After all your father and I have done for you, this is how you repay us? You have hurt us so much. Don't you care about us?

Therapist: Yes, you have been feeling hurt and angry by Bobby's behavior. The anger is coming from a place of care. You care about Bobby and don't understand why he was using drugs. Perhaps you've been feeling conflicted about detaching because it felt like you didn't care or Bobby didn't care about his recovery.

Teresa: Yes, part of me thinks that if Bobby doesn't seem to care, then why should I? But I can't pretend that I don't care. I'm actually beginning to feel nauseated right now.

Therapist: Okay, what thoughts go with the nausea?

Teresa: [Sobbing] If I let go, I have to accept Bobby might die. That's it. Deep down, letting go feels like letting him die. I can't do that.

Therapist: Of course, you love Bobby and want what is in his best interest. Detachment doesn't mean letting go of Bobby. It means letting go of any behavior you were doing that inadvertently accommodated the substance abuse, like giving him money or bailing him out of jail. You can still express love and care toward Bobby in other ways.

Paying attention to what the client is expressing nonverbally or what *you* are experiencing physically provides much more information than what the client is saying with her words. Although the idea of "lovingly detaching" appealed to Teresa's intellectual side, the CARE and ANGER systems in her emotional brain were madly protesting. Anger is a request from the emotional brain to make something in the world stop. Until Teresa's emotional brain could believe detaching was a form of CARING that could help her son stay alive and sober, it wasn't going to buy any positive spin we tried to put on that situation.

I'll go into more detail on how to help the client put words to these physical sensations in Chapter 4, Locating the Root of an Emotional Conflict and Chapter 10, Integrating Mindful Movement. As you map out this visceral awareness of the client's inner experience and guide her to give voice to it in a safe environment, you make implicit beliefs explicit and create a deeper sense of emotional understanding between you and the client. One of Dan Siegel's clients described it as "feeling felt." If you want any credibility in the therapeutic relationship, it's crucial to demonstrate this understanding of the client's tacit feelings and beliefs. After all, if your clients don't think you "get" them, then it doesn't matter how many degrees or certificates hang on your wall. People are only receptive to advice from others who seem to deeply understand their problem and position. Furthermore, as you model nonjudgmental curiosity and acceptance of the client's subconscious material, you model how the client can courageously cultivate the same curiosity and acceptance within herself.

FOLLOWING THE ENERGY

It's easy to empathically connect with clients who are emotionally receptive like Teresa, but how do you emotionally connect with clients who are more guarded, affectively flat, or don't say much at all?

Alex was a quiet, shy, 21-year-old man who came to therapy at the request of his father. He'd failed out of college twice and was deeply depressed. During the intake, Alex said he was motivated for therapy and wasn't just coming to therapy because his dad wanted him to come. Yet, when I asked Alex what he'd like to get out of therapy, he blushed, grinned sheepishly, and said, "I don't know." To stimulate ideas, I threw out a few potential goals such as feeling better about himself, discovering new interests, or getting along with his parents better. Alex paused, and then blankly responded, "Yeah, any of that would be good." Even when I asked open-ended questions such as "What do you like to do for fun?" Alex tilted his head to the side, shrugged his shoulders, and said, "I don't know."

To engage a client, you have to look for signs of energy or "sparks of life," as Ron Taffel (2012) calls it. All clients have a spark of life somewhere, even when they appear to be flat, depressed, or achingly introverted. Like Taffel, I've found if I strike up more of a casual conversation with these cautious clients, their anxiety goes down and a topic that energizes them usually reveals itself. In an effort to provoke a spark of life within Alex, I decided to ask him questions about his job as a grocery store clerk in a way a friend might ask, not a therapist. I was looking for anything that might elicit the slightest bit of emotion or energy so I could figure out what was important to him. The conversation went something like this:

Therapist: Hey Alex, can I ask you something? Would you let someone check out at the express lane if they had 18 items instead of 12?

Alex: Yeah, maybe if there wasn't anyone waiting.

Therapist: Has anyone become angry when you told them they had to go to another line?

Alex: Oh yeah. People do not like it when you tell them that.

Therapist: Well, what do you do when that happens?

Alex: I just try to ignore it and let my manager handle it.

Therapist: I heard that you guys have to scan so many items per minute and can actually get written up if you don't make the quota consistently. Is that true?

Alex: Yes, and it's completely ridiculous. My old manager was not hung up on it, but this new manager is completely anal about it. If I lose my job at a grocery store because I'm not a fast scanner, my parents will really think I'm a loser.

Therapist: So, what do you do? Practice scanning things on your kitchen counter at home with a timer?

Alex: [Laughs] No! Actually, I've asked to be transferred to the produce section. I'm kind of interested in that, especially the organic produce. The manager in that department is nice and I think it's really interesting. I'm growing my own tomatoes this summer. I hate mass-grown tomatoes—yuck!

Therapist: Wow, that's cool! I love fresh vegetables from the garden, but I don't know a thing about growing my own. How did you get started?

Although Alex was still a bit tense and reserved in his speech, his eyes widened and he made more direct eye contact with me as he began to tell me about his tomatoes. I would ask for more and more detail until I could garner a sense of how his day revolved around these plump, red beauties. He brought in photos as the plants grew and beamed as he told me about how he cared for them.

Because the emotional brain responds to metaphors, I planted seeds of inspiration with comments like "Wow, your hard work is really paying off here. . . . Isn't it amazing how you started with the tiniest seed of something and slowly nurtured it into something beautiful?" In another session, Alex temporarily got discouraged because one of his plants died. Later, he salvaged part of the stem, replanted it, and was pleasantly surprised when it sprouted up a few weeks later. I kept with the metaphors, commenting, "So, you were able to salvage something you thought was gone, and within time, it gave way to more growth."

I never explicitly tied the metaphors to anything else in his life. Instead, I've learned if I let the client's subconscious determine how to apply the information, he may do something much more innovative than I could have suggested. For example, within a few months, our shared enthusiasm for Alex's green thumb led him to enroll into a Master Gardener's program. That option would not have occurred to me, but an ad in the newspaper about this program caught Alex's attention. Moreover, he was more committed to the program because it was *his* idea, not a directive from me or his parents.

Many therapists who work with adolescents and young adults know talking about side interests like this often engages youthful clients more than classic therapeutic questioning. Yet I am surprised how often briefly exploring tangential interests enlivens my connection with older clients, too. Although I'd learned the value of integrating free-flowing, natural conversations when working with adolescents in my internship, the protocolized nature of the managed care model caused me to feel like I was "wasting time" if I traversed into these side discussions. Now I know that it's not a waste of time if the client's interests ignite that spark of energy that lights the way out of suffering. I believe it's absolutely therapeutic and provides another way that therapists can recruit positive affective systems to balance and regulate negative emotional systems.

CONNECTING THROUGH PLAY AND MOVEMENT

Sometimes clients aren't so much out of touch with their emotions as they are afraid of their emotions. With these clients, I often invite affective expression through play and movement so they feel less threatened by their emotions. Jeanette was a 45-year-old client who was raped by someone at her workplace. She described herself as a take-charge kind of woman who'd raised two children by herself and worked her way up the corporate ladder into an executive position. Jeanette took charge in our first session, too, making it clear she wasn't looking for any "touchy-feely" type of psychotherapy. She just wanted some practical tools to manage anxiety and put this event behind her quickly. Jeanette said her most troubling symptoms were insomnia and nightmares and asked me to teach her relaxation techniques. Rather than wrestle with Jeanette for control of the session, I obliged her request and let her know that I admired her enthusiasm. I led her into a "calming breath" exercise and noticed she took fast, short inhalations and looked uncomfortable as she held her breath for several seconds as if she was reluctant to exhale. On her fourth inhalation, Jeanette clenched her fists and closed her eyelids tightly as though she were fighting back tears. I felt compelled to reassure and coach her:

Therapist: Jeanette, let's pause for a moment so I can check in with you. What are you noticing within your body as you do this?

Jeanette: My heart is racing. I can't seem to calm down.

Teresa: Okay, that's the kind of feedback I'm looking for. That's actually a physiological response to strengthen you. After a trauma, your mind can confuse relaxation with letting your guard down and so it defends against that. Your heart is beating fast to prepare you to run from a situation that seems weird. It feels even weirder because you're sitting still when your body wants to move. Standing and stretching might actually feel better right now.

I stood up and stretched my arms over my head and twisted from my waist, side to side. My intention was to assist Jeanette in making peace with her body, normalize her feelings, and put a positive perspective on her physical reactions.

Jeanette: [Standing and stretching] Yes. That does feel better.

Therapist: Good. What sensations are you noticing within your body right now?

Jeanette: My heartbeat has slowed down. It feels lighter in my chest. I don't feel on the verge of tears. Ugh, I hate crying. It makes me feel weak.

Therapist: Well, I don't see anybody waving a white flag here. You're standing up to this thing. Emotion is energy trying to get you to do something. The emotion of fear is asking you to move away from something that seems strange or dangerous. Sadness and tears are asking you to pull back, reflect, and express compassion for yourself. No wonder you've been feeling confused. It's like your body is shouting "Run!" but your heart is saying "Slow down, protect me, take care of me."

Jeanette: Yes. I feel so conflicted. I want to fight and run, but I also feel like I could break down at any moment. I hate it. I'm not a crier.

Therapist: Well, if you don't like crying, you can shake that energy off, too, like this. *[I shook around, then shuffled my feet like a boxer as I punched my arms out into the air.]*

Jeanette: [Laughs, and mimics my shuffling]

Therapist: Crying is a lot easier and it looks less ridiculous, but it's up to you.

Jeanette chuckled and actually shuffled around with me before her laughter segued to tears. I offered her my hand and she squeezed it as she let herself cry. In the past I might have encouraged Jeanette to explore what felt scary about crying and why it made her feel weak. Not only would that have increased Jeanette's self-consciousness, but it also would have encouraged more intellectualization. I needed to build more rapport with her before pursuing deeper emotional exploration. I also didn't want her to escape back into her head by attempting to analyze her feelings.

My intention was to give Jeanette a little education about emotion to appeal to her intellectual side, then model dealing with intense emotion by using movement and humor. Goading Jeanette to laugh and play with me discharged the emotional energy in a way that felt less daunting. Initiating playfulness in a session is another great way to build rapport and strengthen the therapeutic alliance. In fact, rats in Panksepp's lab demonstrated more interest, responsiveness, and affection toward the scientists who played with them than toward the scientists who maintained a cold, clinical stance (Panksepp & Biven, 2012). I'll go into more detail on ways to use humor, play, and movement in your sessions in Chapter 8, Priming With Play and Humor, and Chapter 10, Integrating Mindful Movement.

ATTUNING, MISATTUNING, AND REATTUNING

What if Jeanette hadn't responded favorably to my playfulness? I would have just apologized for misreading her and tried something else. Fortunately, we do not have to be in emotional resonance with the client 100% of the time to nurture a strong therapeutic alliance. Most clients are relieved when you notice something didn't click with them and openly invite them to clarify things for you. In her book *Being a Brain-Wise Therapist*, Bonnie Badenoch (2008) acknowledges her patients have said moments of repair in the therapeutic relationship have often "been the most moving" and "prompted a leap forward" in their therapy sessions. Likewise, research on the qualities of a strong therapeutic alliance found that a therapist's admitting to error or self-doubt actually enhanced trust and connection with clients (Niessen-Lie et al., 2010; Norcross, 2010). In any relationship we encounter a process of attunement, misattunement, and reattunement. So, rather than strive for constant attunement, it's more worthwhile to recognize when you've lost attunement, acknowledge it to the client, and do something to get back into attunement.

The best way to do this is to recognize the nonverbal signs of agreement and disagreement between you and the client. When the client is in agreement, you'll notice a slight leaning forward, nodding of the head, eye contact, open body posture, and statements such as "Exactly. That's right. Yes. You got it." (See Figure 2.1 for a photo of nonverbal signs of agreement.)

When you've lost attunement, you'll see the client pull back and notice looks that reflect disagreement such as arms crossed, raised eyebrows, or lips pursed tightly. (See Figure 2.2 for a photo of nonverbal signs of disagreement.) Alternatively, you might see a confused look on the client's face with his eyebrows furrowed, head cocked to the side, or even a leaning in as he turns an ear toward you, as if he didn't hear you correctly.

Sometimes the client will just trail off in her voice or become silent and stare at you blankly as she withdraws. Of course, the client may just say, "Well, that's not really it," or the classic line, "Yes, but . . . " Rather than interpret this as resistance, take it as a sign that there is more to explore and clarify.

Jeanette and I encountered misattunement in our second session. She said, "Since I last saw you, I've been able to relax more during the day, but I'm still replaying this incident in my head at night. I'm tired of thinking about it. I'm ready to be past this."

Figure 2.1 Nonverbal signs of agreement. © Courtney Armstrong

Figure 2.2 Nonverbal signs of disagreement. © Courtney Armstrong

I replied, "I'm glad you've been able to relax more during the day. Tell me more about which aspects of the incident have been replaying in your head. I want to understand so I can help you move past it."

"Um . . ." she said hesitantly, as she leaned away from me. "All of it replays in my head because I want to figure out *how* it happened. One minute I was making copies of the annual report and the next minute—I'm pinned on top of the copy machine by this guy and I can't move. I couldn't even defend myself . . . " Jeanette's voice trailed off and she looked away as her eyes welled up.

I responded, "Okay. I'm following you now. Even though you'd like to be past this, you've also been interested in figuring out how this happened."

Jeanette leaned back in toward me and said, "Yes. I want to understand how he managed to get me in a position where I couldn't move or defend myself. I'm tired of reliving it, but I want to figure out how I could have stopped it."

In my eagerness to help Jeanette heal, I initially locked onto her words "I want to get past this." But her nonverbal language let me know that she was not ready to move forward. She wanted to make sense of what happened first. When I thought back on it, this is also what happened in our first session. Her intellectual side came to the session asking for coping tools, but her emotional side was asking for understanding, reassurance, and support. When in doubt, go with what the nonverbal language is telling you. The body doesn't lie.

One caution: Do not call the client's attention to incongruent body language by saying, "I see you just leaned back and crossed your arms. Is there something you disagree with?" This kind of response facilitates defensiveness and self-consciousness and could cause the client to clam up more. Keep it light and respectful. Just say, "I get the sense that what I'm saying is not resonating with you. What else do I need to understand?" Taking the time to check in and ask the client for this feedback builds trust and rapport and is another quality Norcross found to be essential to therapeutic effectiveness.

PACING AND LEADING

As psychologist Bill Doherty (2012) describes it, therapeutic communication is always a balance of *pacing* and *leading*. Doherty defines *pacing* as following, tracking, attuning, and empathizing with the client. I've mostly focused on the art of pacing in this chapter. The intention of pacing is to attune and build rapport as you gain an understanding of the client's feelings and perceptions. Conveying warmth and acceptance as you bring the client's emotional experiences and implicit beliefs into conscious awareness can be therapeutic in and of itself. But pacing can also be used as a motivating force when it causes the client to better recognize the discrepancy between where he is and where he wants to be.

As my client Teresa got more in touch with her fear of detaching, she realized she needed to find a way to care without enabling her son. When Alex elaborated on his feelings of frustration and boredom as a grocery store clerk, he became aware of a deeper interest to grow his own produce. When I paced with Jeanette's fear of emotional expression, it led her to reclaim her sense of strength and self-compassion.

Yet pacing doesn't always lead to these insights and changes. More often than not, clients have no idea how to get out of the emotional maze that they're in. They are relying on you to lead them out of it. Elaborating on their feelings ad nausea will not get them there. Emotional insight can provide the fuel for change, but without a destination, the engine revs aimlessly or just sits, running idle.

Transitioning from pacing to leading is the trickiest part of communication for most therapists. If you jump too quickly into *leading* with interpretations, solutions, or analysis, you risk losing the emotional connection with your client. Yet if you spend too much time pacing, the therapy feels like it's going nowhere and you can wind up feeling just as exasperated as your clients. In the next chapter, Eliciting Exciting Goals, I'll show you how to create that balance.

CHAPTER 3

Eliciting Exciting Goals

In the last chapter, we focused on ways to enliven the therapeutic alliance with your clients by attuning to both explicit and implicit communication, following their energy, and inviting playfulness and humor into the relationship. This is often referred to as pacing with your client so that he or she feels safe, supported, and understood. Yet, if you spend too much time pacing, therapy can stagnate and leave you and the client both feeling stuck. Then again, if you move too quickly toward setting goals or suggesting solutions, you can encounter resistance from the client. Ideally, you want to pique the client's interest in exploring solutions so that *the client* initiates the movement toward his or her goals. To pivot the therapy in this direction, I recommend using a communication pattern that I call "Align, Lift, and Lead, as described in the following paragraphs."

ALIGNING AND LIFTING

You align with the client's perspective using the responsive attunement skills we discussed throughout the previous chapter. Yet, when stating back your understanding to the client, insert the "*has been*" tense change of the verb. In English, the "has been" tense change is called the past perfect progressive tense of a verb. I learned through my hypnosis training that this tense change also suggests to the *subconscious* that an action has ended or is in the process of ending (Connelly, 2014; O'Hanlon & Beadle, 1997).

For example, recall that my client Teresa essentially said, "I am so angry at Bobby. Doesn't he care about us?"

I replied, "So, you *have been* feeling really hurt and angry by Bobby's behavior. You care about him and don't understand why he was using drugs." This response acknowledges Teresa's feelings, but the slight tense change suggests that she won't have to feel hurt and angry forever and highlights her caring feelings toward Bobby.

Teresa would have also agreed with the statement, "So you are really angry at Bobby and feel like he wouldn't use drugs if he cared about you." But using the present tense of the verb directs her mind to focus on the anger and colludes with her erroneous belief that Bobby intentionally uses drugs to hurt her.

In addition to the "has been" tense change, you want to distinguish feelings and thoughts from the maladaptive meaning the client has attributed to a behavior. Teresa's maladaptive belief was that Bobby didn't care about her; I reframed it to "You care about Bobby and don't understand why he was using drugs." Reframing her question to the factual statement "he was using drugs" avoids interpretation of *why* he hasn't was using and neutralizes the distorted meaning her mind was attaching to Bobby's behavior.

Practice using the "Align, Lift, and Lead" formula by considering a response to this client statement: "I am depressed and I don't know how to pull out of it." Think about what you would say to this client using the "has been" tense change and separating feelings and thoughts from the client's identity.

My response was, "So you *have been* feeling depressed and you're interested in finding a way to pull out of it." First, I used the "has been" tense change, which implies that even though he's been feeling depressed, it doesn't mean he'll continue to feel that way. Second, the client said "I *am* depressed" as if he embodied depression. I wanted to distinguish that he had been *feeling* depressed, as opposed to "being depressed." Third, I incorporated what I call a *lift* in my response when I said, ". . . *and you're interested* in finding a way to pull out of it." I call this a "lift," because it lifts the client's sense of hopefulness and acknowledges a strength he can use to move forward.

To lift, add a brief statement that affirms the client's visible efforts, talents, intelligence, interest, or motivation. This will reinforce the client's sense of competence and the *belief* that he can change. Other examples of statements that "lift" include the following:

- *You're here, so you are obviously motivated to make things better . . .*
- *You're clearly interested in getting a handle on this thing . . .*
- *You recognize that way of thinking about it has not been to your best advantage.*

For more examples, see Worksheet 3.1: Align, Lift, and Lead at the end of this chapter.

LEADING THE CLIENT

While lift statements bolster the client's belief that he or she is capable of change, lead statements suggest how to change or what change might look like. Even though clients want to feel competent enough to solve their problems, they are seeking your leadership and guidance. If they could solve their problems through self-reflection and insight, they wouldn't be sitting in your office. Taking the initiative by tentatively suggesting how the client's thoughts and behavior might change prompts the client to generate ideas, too.

For example, even though Teresa said she wanted to detach from her son's behavior, she'd never conceived of what detachment might actually look like day to day. So I led her by stating, "So, as a result of us working together, I'm seeing you taking better care of yourself, returning to things you enjoy, and discovering positive ways to connect with Bobby, focusing on things that interest both of you."

This approach is different from asking the "miracle question" as is done in solution-focused brief therapy. The miracle question goes something like this: "If you woke up tomorrow feeling more at peace about detaching from your son's substance abuse behavior, what might have changed? How do you suppose you'd be viewing the situation?" Although this question can sometimes generate useful insights, many clients will reply by saying, "I have no idea, lady. That's why I'm here." They're so mired down in the problem they can't fathom what it would be like to be without the problem.

Imagine a guy has fallen into a 12-foot-deep hole and asks you to help him out. The thing to do is throw him a rope and shine a light down in the hole so you can both collaborate on a plan to get him out. You don't start by asking, "Hey, buddy if you weren't in that hole, how do you think you'd be feeling and acting? How do you think you should get out?" While this may be a facetious comparison, the point I want to make is that as a trained therapist, you are the one with the perspective outside the hole and have access to knowledge and resources the client can't reach right now. Throwing your ideas out there is like shining a light and throwing a rope down into the hole. It leads the client to begin conceiving that change is possible.

BALANCING APPEAL AND POSSIBILITY

Of course, there is an art to delivering a lead that will motivate your client. If you make it too grand, the client will think it's unattainable. Yet, if you don't make it compelling enough, it won't elicit the client's interest or motivation. For example, my client Emma asked if our sessions could increase her motivation to lose weight. Emma was 100 pounds overweight and her doctor was urging her to lose at least 50 pounds over the course of a year. Although losing 50 pounds seemed more doable than losing 100 pounds, Emma still found this goal daunting.

Self-efficacy, or the belief one can achieve a goal, is another important aspect of motivation. Albert Bandura's (1977) research most notably demonstrated that if people do not think they are capable of changing a behavior, they are unlikely to put effort into it. Thus, your interventions need to strengthen the client's expectancy that she is capable of change and that it will be worth the effort.

As Emma's doctor attempted to do, you can collaborate with the client to adjust the target goal by breaking it into smaller objectives that seem more attainable. However, Connelly taught me you have to find the right balance between appeal and possibility. For instance, when I said to Emma, "I understand the thought of losing 50 pounds has seemed overwhelming. How does it feel to consider losing just 1 pound per week?"

Emma agreed losing 1 pound per week seemed achievable, but her lackluster facial expressions let me know this goal was not very enticing for her. So I revamped it by adding, "Well, as a result of you and I discovering the strategies that work for you, I'm seeing you 5 pounds lighter, 10 pounds lighter, on the way to still lighter. . ." Emma's face lit up and she nodded her head. The idea of losing 10 pounds had the right amount of allure and possibility for Emma. In addition, she said I piqued her interest by suggesting our sessions would be a process of discovering strategies that worked for her, rather than a process of judging and grading her on her progress.

Phrasing the goal statement with the words, "I'm seeing you . . ." communicates my intention and belief in Emma's ability to change. Even if the client can't envision her success yet, hearing that you believe in her can be very encouraging. In fact, research by Marco Iacoboni and colleagues (2005) has shown that the therapist's intention and belief in the client has a profound impact on the client's success in therapy. Similarly, the developers of motivational interviewing, Miller and Rollnick (2002) found that the therapist's expectation about the client's capacity for change predicts therapy outcomes.

Notice that I didn't put a timetable on how long it would take Emma to lose weight. In fact, if I suggested, "I'm seeing you losing 10 pounds in 2 months," it would've caused her mind to question possibility again. The emotional brain doesn't understand timetables. Remember the emotional brain thinks like an animal. Squirrels do not motivate themselves by thinking, "My goal today is to find 25 nuts in 3 hours." Squirrels are motivated by the sight of the acorns and the aroma of the pecans. Once stimulated in this sensory way, the squirrel's mind quickly creates strategies that will get it to the nuts as soon as possible. Our emotional brains work the same way.

CREATING A SENSORY REPRESENTATION OF A GOAL

Because the SEEKING system in the emotional brain is stimulated through the senses, creating a sensory representation of a goal can ignite motivation. Rather than framing Emma's goal as "I will lose 10 pounds," I guided her to imagine *feeling* stronger and more comfortable in her body; *seeing* herself buying a new shirt and liking how she looks in it; and *hearing* her breath flow more easily as she walked up steps.

In his book *Cognitive-Experiential Theory*, Epstein cites several studies that demonstrate how imagined experience can influence the experiential system in our emotional brains as much as real experience. The emotional brain directs behavior according to the anticipation of positive or negative affect. Thus, it is possible to increase motivation by imagining the joy and satisfaction of behaving a certain way.

Visualizing the desired outcome can get the motivation going, but to really follow through with a plan, you also have to vividly imagine doing the actual behavior that would lead to the desired outcome. For instance, to reinforce her motivation to do the behavior required to lose 10 pounds, Emma focused on appreciating the taste of healthy food, enjoying getting out for a walk each day, and savoring the peace of mind that came from ending her meal before her stomach was uncomfortably full.

My client Saundra, whom I referenced in the Introduction, was not very emotionally motivated until we connected her goals to sensory images of what mattered to her. She was a busy surgeon working in an extremely stressful environment. Although Saundra was very receptive to using biofeedback and mindfulness skills in our sessions, she rarely implemented these skills outside the session. Rather than label this as resistance, we explored obstacles that seemed to get in her way. Saundra explained, "When I'm in your office, it's easy because it's quiet and I can focus. Out there, I am too distracted or worry someone will see me meditating and think I'm sleeping on the job. I can't do it at home because I can't even go to the bathroom without one of my kids walking in on me."

Saundra and I agreed that the initial goal wasn't so much that she meditate for 20 minutes each day, but that she have a way to calm her emotions and quiet her ruminating thoughts. As I discussed earlier in this chapter, you often have to suggest to the client what her desired state of mind might look, sound, or feel like. Using a symbolic imagery technique I learned from Connelly's Rapid Resolution Therapy (RRT) model, I prompted Saundra by suggesting, "Let's think of your mind working this way for a moment—calm, secure, focused, feeling grateful you helped improve someone's health, or coming home from a long day and enjoying a smile from one of your children." Saundra closed her eyes, released a soft smile, and said, "Okay, I'm getting it."

"Now," I instructed, "let's create a symbol that would represent your mind working that way, something in nature or an animal in the wild. What comes to mind?"

Saundra sat silently with her eyes closed for a moment and said, "The sun just beginning to rise over the lake I told you about where I go running some mornings. I like it when it is still a little dark and quiet outside. The colors in the sky are kind of muted, like these sheer pink-violets and soft peachy-yellows."

"Beautiful," I replied, "so see that sunrise and take a deep breath in, pause for a moment . . . and release as you exhale. Saundra continued the imagery for three breath cycles, then opened her eyes and said, "That was nice. I feel calmer. Having an image to focus on helps, otherwise my mind is all over the place."

Obtaining an image that was personally meaningful for Saundra not only provided her with a handy tool for reducing her anxiety but also served the purpose of increasing her motivation and sense of self-efficacy because *she* was able to identify an ideal symbol. Saundra also noted that she felt more motivated to decrease her anxious habits when she considered it would be a loving thing to do for her children, rather than doing it for herself or her coworkers. Again, this illustrates the goal has to be linked to something emotionally compelling and intrinsically motivating for the client. We'll discuss more ways to use inspirational imagery for motivation and healing in Chapter 6.

IDENTIFYING INTRINSIC MOTIVATORS

In his book *Effective Techniques for Treating Resistant Clients*, Clifton Mitchell stated, "People do not change because of logic. People change when they have an emotionally compelling reason to change" (2007, p. 16). Furthermore, Mitchell opines that many people come to therapy because they don't like the status quo, but haven't conceptualized something they would desire more. Thus, the therapist's job is to draw out the deep-seated desires that will innately motivate the client. Likewise, Miller and Rollnick (2002), repeatedly state that constructive behavior change occurs when the client connects the change to "something cherished, deeply important to them, and close to their hearts." In other words, people aren't so much driven by external rewards as they are by intrinsic rewards or believing the pursuit itself will be inherently rewarding, fun, or worthwhile.

To determine what innately motivates your clients, *follow their energy*. As I mentioned in Chapter 2, notice the topics that elicit enthusiasm in your client's voice, broaden affect in her face, or increase animation in her body language. What does she get excited about? What does she most care about? What evokes tears of joy or touches her heart? You could also explore what really ticks her off, but you've got to get beneath the anger to reveal the value or truth that is important to her. Taking the time to explore and develop the client's dreams, values, and interests positively pivots the client's energy toward something more compelling than her pain.

For example, in Chapter 2 my client Alex was rather flat in his interaction with me until we started discussing his interest in growing tomato plants. When I saw his eyes light up as he gushed over these plants, I knew this horticultural interest could be the fulcrum of his recovery. To set the stage for making this part of the treatment plan, I used the following align, lift, and lead statements: "Even though you've been feeling depressed, cultivating these tomato plants obviously brings you energy and joy. I think it's great for you to spend time each day with those plants, Alex. It's like a natural antidepressant for you."

Bringing Alex's awareness to the delight his tomatoes brought him and suggesting his first goal could be spending daily time with his plants was much more intriguing for him than focusing on the symptoms of depression. Moreover, using this natural interest inevitably brought up plenty of teachable moments. For example, when one of his plants died, it gave us an opportunity to discuss how to cope adaptively with disappointment and feelings of failure. When his parents chided him for spending so much time with his plants, it gave us the opportunity to look at how to deal with criticism and communicate more effectively with his parents.

Considering Panksepp's concept of our primary emotional systems, I believe centering treatment around something enjoyable and personally meaningful to the client stimulates the SEEKING and PLAY emotional systems, both of which Panksepp believes can lead a person out of a depressed state. Furthermore, as we've discussed throughout the book, the emotional brain learns not by reason but through a specific *experience* that enables it to apply new skills.

ENCOURAGING AUTONOMY, MASTERY, AND PURPOSE

Of course, many clients aren't going to have an enjoyable hobby like Alex that can be used to leverage them out of depression. However, most people feel inspired by any activity that gives them a sense of autonomy, mastery, and purpose. Daniel Pink, author of *Drive: The Surprising Truth of What Motivates Us* (2009), found these three qualities to be the most important for triggering intrinsic motivation.

In regard to autonomy, people need to feel in control of what they do, when they do it, and how they do it. Although the therapist can elicit goals that interest the client, it's best to let the client determine how he or she is going to pursue those goals. The client may still need your coaching in terms of setting realistic objectives, breaking goals into manageable tasks, and staying the course when things get tough. The therapist's task is to present options only as a means of prompting the client's creativity and generativity. People are much more likely to follow through on a task if they think it's their idea. That's fine with me! Whatever gets the client moving is the initial goal. The second goal is sustaining the momentum as the client encounters obstacles on the road to change.

People are inherently motivated to get better at something that matters to them. But mastery takes hard work, commitment, and patience. Interestingly, when someone is mastering something, he is more responsive to encouragement of his persistence than to praise for the outcome (Dweck, 2006). Thus, it's your job to reinforce the client's efforts and perseverance as he implements new skills and connect it to the client's values. People tend to be more invested in a goal when they believe it is contributing to a cause, upholds a deeply held ethic, or connects them to something larger than themselves.

My client Jeanette was inspired when we found ways to tie her goals to an increased sense of autonomy, mastery, and purpose. Recall that Jeanette was the client in Chapter 2 who had been raped and wanted to return to her usual confident, goal-driven self. I gleaned from our conversations that Jeanette really enjoyed the feeling of mastering something. For example, in one session she told me: "I overcame my fear of heights by bungee jumping. I continued horseback riding even after a horse threw me off its back. I have never let something paralyze me like this."

The sexual assault also caused Jeanette to reevaluate her life. In spite of her accomplishments, Jeanette said she suddenly felt empty and concluded her life lacked deep purpose or meaning. I decided to appeal to Jeanette's desire for mastery by suggesting that treatment could focus on developing her prowess in mindfulness, focusing, and imagery skills. After all, I explained to Jeanette, martial arts masters and Olympic athletes have to cultivate these psychological skills no matter how knowledgeable, strong, or talented they are. Jeanette liked this idea. She didn't want sympathy as much as she wanted to transform her traumatic experience into something that could strengthen her and repurpose her life.

As we explored activities that might renew her sense of purpose, Jeanette realized she had a passionate interest in mentoring young women. She'd considered volunteering for an organization that connects professionals with college students who are looking for mentors. However, Jeanette was surprised to find she felt more emboldened after learning of an organization that helps women who have been victims of sex trafficking. Assisting these women in reclaiming their lives was immensely rewarding for Jeanette.

REVEALING INTERNAL CONFLICTS

What if the client has identified a clear emotionally compelling goal but still feels blocked or lacks the belief she can achieve it? Emotional conflicts and ambivalence about pursuing what is desired are common. In fact, ambivalence is the essence of "stuckness," and this internal conflict is essentially what brings clients to therapy. You can expect that as soon as you clarify the client's desire, his internal conflict about having it is going to present itself. This is why I clarify the client's deepest desires first. It not only gets clients more invested in the therapy process, but it more quickly reveals the implicit beliefs and emotional conflicts that have been holding them back.

For example, when Teresa and I began to develop a vision of what healthy detachment from her son's substance abuse would actually look like, her deeper fear that he would die if she detached immediately surfaced. There was a legitimate reason for Teresa to have that fear: Her brother died from substance abuse when he was a young adult. At some level Teresa believed her brother wouldn't have died if her parents had been more involved with his attempts at recovery. Thus, her emotional brain equated detachment with death. No wonder she felt resistance to detaching.

In the next section of the book, I will guide you how to identify the emotional conflicts and implicit beliefs that keep your clients from moving forward in Chapter 4. Then, in Chapter 5, I will show you a process to quickly clear emotional blocks and update implicit patterns at both conscious and unconscious levels.

WORKSHEET 3.1: Align, Lift, and Lead Language Hints

I. Make It a "Has Been"

When reflecting back your understanding of the problem to the client, use the "has been" tense change. This implies to the emotional brain that an ongoing action has ended.

- *There has been a feeling of . . . (depression, anxiety, guilt, etc.)*
- *You're thinking on this has been . . .*
- *You have been through a lot of incredibly tough stuff.*
- *Your mind has been questioning things, even though you recognize you did what came to you to do and it made sense then.*

II. Separate Feelings, Behaviors, and Thoughts From the Person's Identity

People will say, "I'm angry," "I'm a loser," "I can't get past it," "I'm out of control," and so on." Empower the person by talking in terms of thoughts/feelings instead of "you."

- *There's been a whole bunch of anger around that.*
- *Troubling, unhelpful thoughts have been showing up that you realize are not in your best interest.*
- *So this thing happened. It was disturbing and it's not been clear how to get past it.*
- *So much has been going on that it felt out of control.*

III. Lift and Lead

Add a word, phrase, or statement to your reflection that acknowledges the client's strengths, engenders hope, and leads the client in the direction he or she would like to be going.

- *There's been a whole bunch of anger around this situation and that's been getting in the way of you feeling secure, at ease, doing things that are beneficial and useful.*

- *Even though you've had these troubling thoughts/feelings, you're obviously smart and motivated and it's great you're here.*
- *So that experience was really disturbing and you'd like to move beyond it, so it doesn't affect you like that anymore.*
- *Even though (eating, drinking, smoking, cutting, etc.) temporarily relieved those troubling feelings, you recognize doing that stuff hasn't been to your best advantage.*

PART II

HEALING EMOTIONAL WOUNDS

CHAPTER 4

Locating the Root of an Emotional Conflict

No matter how externally motivated clients seem, they often struggle with internal conflicts that prevent them from reaching their goals. In fact, it is this inner dilemma that usually brings people to therapy. How many times have clients said to you, "I know I need to . . . (exercise, stop drinking, assert myself, date nicer people, etc.), but I just can't get myself to do it"? Moreover, how many times have you had these feelings yourself?

As much as a person consciously desires to change a behavior, earlier emotional learning has the ability to override his or her conscious intentions. Even if a person practices a new behavior repeatedly, an old automatic pattern can still take over if its root is not fully identified and updated.

Phobias are a good example of this. Although exposure techniques can decrease fear responses in most situations, fear researchers have found learned fears are rarely 100% extinguished with exposure techniques alone. If you attempt to teach your brain new patterns without clearing the original pattern at its source, you essentially have created two separate learned pathways. For instance, in the case of a phobia of snakes, you've created one pathway that's not associated with fear when you're around snakes voluntarily, but you still may have the old pathway that triggers fear when a snake pops up unexpectedly.

Neuroscientists have only recently determined the key to fully extinguishing and updating old learning. It began 15 years ago in LeDoux's neuroscience lab at New York University when a young graduate assistant named Karim Nader realized that every time you bring up a memory you have an opportunity to change it (Nader, 2012). The trick is you have to update the memory within a few minutes to a few hours of recollecting it. This time window is when a memory "reconsolidates" or gets reprocessed and restored. Before I get into the details of how to update a memory within this time window, you'll need to know how to identify a specific emotional memory for you and your client to reconsolidate. In addition, you'll need to determine the latent meaning that got attached to the emotional memory because it's these implicit, embodied beliefs that are usually maintaining an ongoing pattern.

For example, John was a 48-year-old man who was frustrated by an unexplainable apprehension he felt when disagreeing with his father. John described his father as a reasonable man who did not seem to mind if someone had a different opinion, yet John avoided contradicting his dad in any way. Using the methods I'll show you in this chapter, John recalled a memory of his father, a handball champion, hurling a squeaking mouse against the kitchen wall with one fell swoop of his hand. In addition, John recalled another memory of his dad lobbing a strike to John's face when John smarted off to him as a teenager. John's father later apologized for hitting him so hard and never hit him again, but John still felt uneasy around his dad.

As we explored the implicit meaning John's mind attached to these childhood experiences, he realized, "On some level I guess I got the impression that if you cross my dad, he'll wallop you!" Prior to this exploration, John hadn't consciously thought about those events in years. After we brought these memories and their meanings into John's conscious awareness and updated them at the experiential-emotional level, John was much more comfortable talking with his father.

Maladaptive reactions like John's are typically formed in response to prior emotionally charged events. When an event happens that involves intense emotional arousal, emotion acts like glue that sears the experience into a learned pathway instantly, so it doesn't require a lot of repetition. Your mind probably did the same thing when you first touched a hot stove. This indelible learning is meant to protect you and prevent you from putting yourself into harm's way.

Often, the process of taking events from our past and putting them into proper context happens over time without therapy. For instance, you learned not to touch a stove when it was hot but realized you didn't have to avoid stoves altogether. When we put an event into this conscious context, it is called an *explicit memory*. An explicit memory is a memory we can retrieve consciously and describe without a lot of emotional arousal because we've stored it within an adaptive framework. On the other hand, *implicit memory* is memory that is stored as more of a felt experience that hasn't been fully integrated into a current context, time, or space. Implicit memories involve behavioral learning, emotional reactions, and bodily sensations that lack the feeling of coming from the past. As far as the emotional brain is concerned, the behavior you used to survive an unresolved event is still relevant and necessary for your survival.

Why do some memories stay locked in this implicit state? When an event triggers intense emotional arousal, like extreme fear or anger, the emotional brain will dominate the brain's resources to deal with it. The amygdala assesses whether a stimulus is threatening and activates the fight-flight-or-freeze response while temporarily inhibiting activity in the hippocampus and prefrontal cortex. During such an emotionally charged event, processing in the amygdaloid system receives precedence, because emotional systems need access to as much glucose and circuits in the brain as possible to mobilize a response. Thus, an emotionally charged memory can remain stored in a felt sense at the affective level without getting explicitly linked up to adaptive information that comes through the hippocampus and prefrontal cortex. This is why you may rationally understand that you no longer need to feel afraid of a trigger from the past, yet still react as emotionally as you did back then.

LOCATING A RELEVANT EMOTIONAL MEMORY

To locate the emotional memory at the root of a recurring affective or behavioral pattern, I use a technique I learned years ago in my hypnosis training called the Affect Bridge. John G. Watkins, founder of ego-state therapy developed this technique in 1971. Since then many therapy models have incorporated similar approaches for locating implicit memories. For example, those of you trained in eye movement desensitization and reprocessing (EMDR) may recognize this as the Affect Scan or Floatback technique (Shapiro, 2001). Coherence therapy and holographic reprocessing integrate similar protocols using the terms "discovery experience" and "experiential discovery," respectively. Likewise, Dan Siegel (2010a) uses the acronym SIFT as he guides clients to do a body scan for Sensations, Images, Feelings, and Thoughts associated with memories or somatic symptoms. I've outlined the gist of the Affect Bridge technique here. For easy reference see Worksheet 4.1, Locating Embodied Beliefs, at the end of this chapter.

The Affect Bridge Technique (inspired by Watkins, 1971)

1. **Recall a recent situation that triggered the undesired response briefly.** The client only needs to bring up the undesired feelings for a minute or so, just enough to recall the associated emotion, sensations, and reactions to conscious awareness at a level that feels tolerable.
2. **What sensations do you feel in your body as you recall the emotional response to this event?** Focusing awareness on the physical sensations tunes the client into the right hemisphere and the way the emotional experience is encoded at the nonverbal, sensory level.
3. **What words or thoughts come to mind as you focus on the sensations in your body associated with this emotional response?** Exploring beliefs associated with the physical *sensations* is more reliable than using the rational mind to intellectualize about the event. I'll explain why later in this chapter.
4. **Let those sensations carry you back to an earlier time in your life when you can first remember having similar feel-**

ings, sensations, or thoughts. Tracing the nonverbal sensations back to an event that provoked similar feelings generally leads to more accurate identification of related memories.

Sometimes only vague images or impressions come to the client's mind rather than a specific event. This is because implicit memories can be encoded as fragments that aren't really linked up as a coherent narrative yet. Guide the client in piecing the images and impressions together by estimating his age at the time of the event, the people who were present, where he was, his best guess as to what happened, or what was said.

You'll know when the client has identified a pertinent memory because there will be a visceral, affective response on the client's face when he or she recalls it. However, unlike Watkins instructed in the 1970s, we now know it is not necessary for the client to fully relive the memory to resolve it. In fact, such abreaction can trigger hyperarousal or hypoarousal of the nervous system in the form of flashbacks and dissociation, which prevents the hippocampus from integrating implicit memory into explicit context (Siegel, 2010b; van der Kolk, 2006). Instead, guide your client to maintain dual awareness of the present moment and stay within a level of arousal that feels tolerable as he or she scans somatic sensations for a related event.

In addition, to avoid creating "false memories," reassure your client that you're only exploring for ways she may have experienced and interpreted a past event. This is not a factual investigation. All memory is subjective and is rarely a full, accurate, factual representation of what actually happened. For instance, policemen will tell you that if there are six eyewitnesses at a car accident, then they'll get six different stories of what occurred. None of the eyewitness reports will match up exactly because we all have different vantage points and filters through which we perceive events. At this point, explain to your client that she's just looking for structural similarity between events. You can get the verbal left hemisphere involved in fact checking and clarifying details later.

Julie's Painful Meals

My client Julie is a good example of how this process works. She was a 25-year-old woman who presented with multiple digestive issues that her doctors labeled psychosomatic because they couldn't find a physical explanation for her symptoms. She called me in desperation because her weight was down to 91 pounds and her family and psychologist had threatened to admit her to the hospital for treatment of anorexia nervosa. Julie did not think she had anorexia. She assured me that she wanted to eat and gain weight because she was hungry and hated feeling so weak and skinny. Her previous psychologist demanded that Julie use painful exposure techniques and self-talk to make herself eat in spite of Julie's difficulty swallowing and digesting anything besides crackers. Though her psychologist was well intentioned, these techniques didn't work for Julie and seemed to exacerbate her feelings of helplessness and shame.

Julie knew that I specialized in treating trauma and thought there may be repressed feelings driving her symptoms, but she couldn't consciously identify a clear trauma from her past. I asked her to tune into the choking sensations in her throat and follow them back to the first time she could remember having a similar feeling.

Within a few minutes, Julie's eyes widened and she actually coughed as she said, "When I was 16 years old sitting at my parent's dinner table. My parents were bitterly arguing and my brother suddenly attacked me. Then my mom joined in and everyone directed their anger towards me. I don't remember exactly what was said or what everyone was arguing about. I just remember my throat closed up and I felt like I was going to throw up. So I ran to the bathroom. The arguing went on for months, until it got to the point I couldn't eat at the dinner table. The only food I could get down was a box of crackers I hid in my bedroom. Later, we discovered my parents had been planning to get a divorce, which was the real source of the family tension, not me. But it felt like everyone blamed me for all our problems."

Prior to this exploration, Julie had no idea what started her difficulty eating. But by tracing the physical sensations back to a related memory, we got to it within a few minutes. Remember the emotional brain speaks through the body and right hemisphere, not in words. The rational mind and verbal left hemisphere want to interpret feelings and sensations but often get the interpretation wrong.

Let me give you an example from a split-brain research study that illustrates the left hemisphere's tendency to confabulate when it encounters something it doesn't understand. In the 1970s neuroscientist Mike Gazzaniga and colleagues conducted investigations with subjects whose corpus callosum had been severed to mitigate epileptic seizures. The corpus callosum is the main area of the brain that integrates right hemispheric and left hemispheric processing. One of the experiments instructed the split-brain subjects to watch different images flash on a screen simultaneously to the left and to the right. The subjects were then asked to use their left and right hands to select two images from a row of picture cards that best matched the photos on the screen.

One subject was presented with an image of a chicken claw on the right side of the screen and a snow-covered house on the left side of the screen. Because the left hemisphere controls the right side of the body, his right eye saw the image of the chicken claw and his right hand pointed to a card with a picture of a chicken head. Because the right hemisphere controls the left side of the body, his left eye saw the snow-covered house and his left hand pointed to a card with a picture of a snow shovel. When the researchers asked the man why he picked these particular picture cards, he replied, "Well, I picked the chicken head because I'm looking at a picture of a chicken claw, so I guess I picked the shovel to clean out the chicken shed!" (Gazzaniga, 2002).

What happened here? Researchers concluded that the left hemisphere did not know what the right hemisphere saw and had no idea why the left hand picked the shovel. So the subject's rational mind made an interpretation based on what the left hemisphere saw (chicken claw) without consciously realizing what the right hemisphere saw (snow-covered house).

This same error can happen when we use our rational minds to search for reasons to explain our behavior. Even though clients may consciously identify a memory that is germane to their situation, I always ask them to check in through their emotional and physical sensations as well. At times, this extra step has led to very surprising discoveries. For instance, one client consciously thought a past rape was the reason for her social anxiety. Yet, when I asked her to follow the somatic sensations associated with her social anxiety back to a memory, an event from third grade emerged in which a bunch of friends embarrassed her in front of the class. Turns out, this experience of feeling like her friends betrayed her was the original source of her social anxiety. Once we reprocessed this particular childhood memory, her anxiety remitted.

EXTRACTING EMBODIED BELIEFS

Ironically, I find the "small-T" traumas frequently have more of a haunting, insidious effect than the "Big-T traumas." With a Big-T trauma like disaster, war, or rape, clients often have greater ability to recognize that they did not cause the event and did what they did in order to survive. On the other hand, small-T traumas usually involve a perceived attachment breach in an important relationship such as rejection, betrayal, engulfment, or neglect. With these types of attachment ruptures, people often feel that *they* were the cause of someone else's behavior.

Sadly, the effects of these so-called small-T traumas aren't small at all. Clients impacted by attachment traumas often present with recurring feelings of shame, guilt, self-loathing, anxiety, or depression without being able to identify a clear cause. Likewise, they often believe they are inherently unworthy, unlovable, defective, or just plain "bad" without understanding why. I call these *embodied beliefs* because they show up as more of a felt sense, rather than as rational thoughts. My clients and I began using the term "embodied beliefs" 12 years ago when I worked in a physician's office treating people with anxiety and psychosomatic issues. For these clients, following their physical sensations back to earlier memories and discovering associated implicit beliefs provided astonishing insight and relief. Rather than being afraid of their symptoms, they got curious about them and the messages their bodies were attempting to communicate. In her book *Holographic Reprocessing* (2005), psychologist Lori Katz believes relationship violations actually form an experiential hologram with programmed emotional and behavioral responses that get reenacted when the person encounters anything similar to the original event. Katz notes the implicit beliefs attached to these experiences become someone's "personal truth," which drives recurring compensating, avoidance, and motivational patterns in the person's life. Katz distinguishes four core violations that can form such experiential holograms and patterns: (1) Neglect, (2) Rejection/Disapproval, (3) Betrayal, and (4) Endangerment.

Neglect occurs when a child's basic emotional, psychological, or physical needs are not responded to or recognized. People who grow up with recurring neglect experiences are often sensitive to feeling ignored, deprived, or abandoned. The essence of their implicit beliefs is "*I don't matter. I am not important. My feelings don't count. People don't care about me. People will leave. Life is hard.*"

Rejection or disapproval violations occur when a young person feels constantly criticized, judged, or ridiculed. Frequent beliefs that crop out of these experiences include, "*I'm not good enough. I'm incompetent. I'm wrong. I'm shameful. People are judgmental. People can't be pleased. Life is against me.*"

Betrayal violations occur when a person feels deceived, manipulated, or when confidences and promises are broken. Common beliefs that develop from betrayal experiences include, "*I'm not loved. I am not valued. I'm stupid. I can't trust my judgment. People can't be trusted. People lie. People use you. Life is unfair.*"

Endangerment occurs when a person is threatened, intimidated, or physically harmed by violence. People who grow up in these circumstances often feel an impending sense of doom and believe the world can be a chaotic, foreboding place to live. The beliefs that a person can internalize from endangerment include, "*I'm bad. It's my fault. If I please them, they won't hurt me. People are dangerous. Life is chaotic.*"

In addition to these four types of attachment violations, I would add a category of "Engulfment" violations in which the boundaries between the child's feelings and the parent's feelings are blurred. Children of narcissistic or extremely dependent parents experience these boundary violations as intrusiveness, enmeshment, or exploitation. As a result, they often have difficulty distinguishing between their needs and the needs of another. The associated beliefs may show up as a codependent traits such as "*Your needs are my needs. My feelings aren't as important as your feelings. I need to feel needed to feel alive and worthwhile. Separation means I don't love you.*" At the other extreme, people raised under these circumstances might present with a distant, avoidant orientation and beliefs like "*If I get close to you, I lose myself. People are needy. People will engulf and then you won't exist.*" Last, people raised in these conditions may develop narcissistic traits themselves with beliefs such as "*I only exist if I am admired. You are an extension of me. My needs should be your needs. If you disagree with me, then I don't exist.*"

When implicit beliefs are articulated, they will typically comprise five words or less, such as "*I am bad. I am unworthy. I don't matter.*" People often feel embarrassed verbalizing these belief statements because they sound so irrational and childish. Reassure the client that the beliefs are stored this way because the emotional brain processes information like an animal or small child and has rudimentary language ability. It learns from experiences, not verbal reasoning.

To unearth the root of an embodied belief, use the Affect Bridge technique I described earlier and guide the client to trace the physical sensations associated with shame, helplessness, or self-loathing back to a potentially unresolved emotional memory. Once you identify a relevant memory, then assist the client in unveiling and articulating the implicit belief that got attached to the event. Julie's embodied beliefs were, "*People can't be trusted. I'm not loved. Another man is leaving . . . and that's a hard thing to swallow.*" She then realized her problems with swallowing surfaced after she and her husband separated and her in-laws blamed her for their marital problems—just like her family of origin did when her parents were getting a divorce.

If a client has difficulty locating feelings, physical sensations, or a related memory, do not pressure her. Instead, teach her self-soothing skills such as mindful breathing, grounding, and positive imagery techniques first. If you are not aware of ways to teach your clients self-soothing skills, I give examples of several tools you can use in Chapters 5–10. Once the client feels like she has a way to self-soothe and calm her nervous system, you can ask the client to list six to ten of the most challenging emotional events she's experienced in her lifetime. Then, you can briefly explore these events with the client to see which incident might have emotional relevance to the current situation. Or use Worksheet 4.1, Locating Embodied Beliefs at the end of this chapter.

Ian's Message: "Don't Believe in Anything"

My client Ian is a good example of how an embodied belief can infiltrate every aspect of someone's life. He was an intelligent 36-year-old engineer who had a precocious sense of humor and was also a talented saxophonist. Yet he struggled with paralyzing panic attacks, depression, and alcoholism that kept him from performing, dating, and even spending time with friends. As we explored the source of his troubles, Ian couldn't identify a concrete event that prompted his symptoms. He said he'd been struggling with anxiety and depression since he was a teenager. He began drinking in his 20s and realized he used alcohol to avoid the feelings of loneliness, self-loathing, and despair that crept up on him nightly.

I asked Ian if he could pull up some of the feelings of loneliness and self-loathing in a session to see if we could trace it back to a particular event. At first he protested and said, "Are you serious? No way. I hate that feeling. I want you to tell me how to get rid of it."

Realizing I needed to remind him of how to use self-soothing skills I'd taught him earlier, I suggested, "Okay. Let's do something else first. Remember how you told me you felt when you were playing your saxophone? Bring to mind one of those times when you were really getting into it, breathing through the rhythm, enjoying the movement of your hands and fingers as the notes formed automatically, and that outside noise just fades away. . ."

Ian closed his eyes, nodded his head, and smiled. "Yeah, that's an amazing feeling. You know I feel isolated from people, but when I'm playing my sax, I feel grounded and connected to the world somehow." He stayed with this reverie a few more minutes, then opened his eyes and said, "That's a good feeling. It feels warm in my chest now, not so hollow and empty."

"Beautiful," I echoed. "Now that you have a way to diminish those negative feelings, let's see if we can clear the source so they stop haunting you."

Ian narrowed his eyes and glared at me teasingly, and then said, "I was afraid you were going to say that. Okay, you want me to tune into that bad feeling and see if I can associate some kind of childhood memory with it?" Ian closed his eyes and furrowed his brow. Within moments his affect became visibly sullen and he swallowed hard.

"Okay," I encouraged, "it looks like you got something. What's coming up?" Ian shrugged and said, "All I can think of is the day my dad left us. I was 12 years old."

"Alright, I'm going to ask you a series of questions that will help us illuminate what's attached to that event. Or I can give the questions to you on a worksheet for you to write out your answers. Respond with the first thing that comes to mind, whether it makes sense or not.

Ian held his hand out and said, "Let me look at the worksheet. It's probably easier for me to write it down." Following are Ian's responses about his feelings of despair.

Ian's Worksheet for Locating Embodied Beliefs

A. Current Problem/Situation

1. The current undesired response occurs when *I'm alone at night.*
2. When I'm in this situation, I feel *despair, hopelessness, self-hatred.*
3. When I have these feelings, I notice these sensations in my body *pit in the bottom of my stomach, hollow or heavy feelings in my chest.*

4. And I have these thoughts: I am *worthless*, others *don't care*, and life is *pointless*.
5. To avoid these feelings and thoughts, I *drink*.

B. Earlier Emotional Memories

6. When I trace these feelings and thoughts back to an earlier time in my life, it reminds me of when *my dad left*.
7. And I had these feelings *anger, confusion, helplessness, hopelessness*.
8. Because it gave me the impression that I *didn't matter*, others *don't care*, and life was *meaningless*.
9. I dealt with it by *destroying my instruments, skipping school, withdrawing*.
10. The advantage of responding this way was *I decided not to believe in anything so I couldn't get hurt or disappointed*.
11. The disadvantage of responding this way is *I feel awful. I disappoint friends who want to hang out with me. My life feels like it has no meaning or purpose*.
12. What I'd like to think and feel now is that *I can have a meaningful life. Having a relationship means something and is worth it, even if I get hurt or disappointed*.

As I read through Ian's answers, I said, "Yes, this makes sense to me. What do you make of it?"

Ian clenched his jaw, threw his head back, and snapped, "What do I make of it? My dad left and I felt *angry and hopeless* because it meant *I didn't matter. He didn't care*. The message I got about the world was *don't believe in anything*. Family doesn't matter. Relationships don't matter. Your accomplishments don't matter. So don't put yourself out there because it doesn't make a damn bit of difference. Nobody cares and you'll just get disappointed."

His face reddened and his eyes began to well up with tears. He buried his head in his hands, and then wiped his face with the sleeve of his shirt as he professed, "Whoa! I didn't know I felt that way. That's it though. I avoid relationships. I avoid pursuing goals. I avoid enjoying anything because, frankly, I don't believe in anything."

Once Ian got in touch with this embodied belief, his therapy took a turn. We were able to reprocess painful memories from his childhood, and he began to believe the process of recovery and pursuing relationships was worthwhile, even if he sometimes experienced pain and disappointment.

The Adaptiveness of a Response

You'll notice on Worksheet 4.1 that I include a statement that asks the person to list the advantage of responding the way he or she did to the past event. I reassure clients that whatever constructs the emotional brain built in response to an emotional event were adaptive at one time. This is why the client has been feeling internal conflicts and the pattern has not changed. Ian's unconscious decision not to believe in anything seemed to protect him from further pain and disappointment. For Julie, having gastrointestinal distress got her out of being picked on and enduring family conflicts. Some therapists might label Julie's response as "secondary gain," because she seems to get a benefit out of remaining sick. Yet I think this label is often used in a derogatory way and implies the client prefers to maintain the status quo over getting well. Katz (2005) suggests looking at problematic responses or behaviors as a *compensating strategy* the client developed to deal with a difficult situation, and I agree. The only reason the behavior hasn't changed is because the client is unaware of a more effective strategy for dealing with the issue.

Similarly, the founders of coherence therapy (CT) believe the client's presenting symptom(s) consist of a well-defined solution to the original problem. In their *Coherence Therapy Manual*, CT founders, Ecker and Hulley described it as the pro-symptom position (PSP) and stated the PSP consists of "linked nonconscious, nonverbal constructs that are perceptual, emotional, somatic, and kinesthetic knowings; knowings one doesn't know one knows until they are made conscious and verbalized" (2011, p. 5). In other words, the PSP is largely unconscious and stored in a felt sense. Until the client becomes consciously aware of the latent necessity of maintaining the symptom, it is unlikely the symptoms and associated responses will change.

To summarize, even though clients come to therapy because they want change, prior unconscious emotional learning may prevent them from moving forward. As irrational as the client's beliefs, behaviors, or emotional responses seem, they were likely to have been adaptive at one time. To update these patterns and beliefs, it's often necessary to locate the original memories where the behavior was learned or reinforced. To do this, guide the client to trace the somatic sensations associated with the unwanted pattern back to an earlier memory where he or she had similar feelings. Worksheet 4.1 can be used by you and the client for this purpose.

In the next chapter I'll go into more depth about how to update and change these unwanted patterns with a five-step process that is based on neuroscience discoveries regarding memory reconsolidation. This process works rather quickly and can be integrated into a variety of theoretical approaches and practice settings.

WORKSHEET 4.1: Locating Embodied Beliefs

A. Current Problem/Situation

1. The current undesired response occurs when ________________
   ____.
2. When I'm in this situation, I feel ________________________
   ____.
3. And I notice these sensations in my body ________________
   ____.
4. And it feels as if I am ____________________________
   ______, other people ________________________, and life is
   ____.
5. To avoid these feelings and thoughts, I ________________
   ____.

B. Earlier Emotional Memories

6. When I trace these sensations, feelings, or thoughts back to an earlier time in my life, it reminds me of when________________
   ____.
7. And I had these feelings ____________________________
   ____.
8. Because it gave me the impression that I ________________
   ____________, other people ________________________,
   and life is ____.
9. I dealt with it then by________________________________
   ____.
10. The advantage of responding this way was ________________
    ____
    ____.
11. The disadvantage of responding this way was________________
    ____
    ____.
12. What I'd like to feel and think now is____________________
    ____
    ____.

CHAPTER 5

Reversing Trauma With Memory Reconsolidation

Can you erase a fear? Until recently, researchers weren't sure. Though we have had moderate success teaching clients how to regulate emotional responses with mindfulness, exposure, and other cognitive-behavioral techniques, most people can only reliably employ these counteractive techniques when they are at a mild to moderate level of emotional arousal.

Furthermore, research indicates that traditional exposure therapy doesn't completely eliminate a fear. We've only recently learned that extinction training must be delivered in a particular way during a specific window of time for exposure to work. Neuroscientists call this process of rewriting and restoring a remembered experience "memory reconsolidation." This chapter will get you up to speed on the memory reconsolidation research and provide you with a simple five-step reconsolidation process to clear an emotional pattern at its root.

THE DISCOVERY OF MEMORY RECONSOLIDATION

Up until 1999, targeting a therapy that could actually change the original properties of a learned fear seemed impossible. Once the synaptic connections of an emotionally charged memory became stabilized, or consolidated, the associated learning appeared to be permanent. Yet, at the turn of the century, a surge of research suggested the emotional valence of a memory could be reversed or changed (see Alberini, 2013; Ecker, Ticic, & Hulley, 2012; and Schwabe, Nader, & Preussner, 2014 for a full literature review).

Karim Nader, one of the neuroscientists advancing this research, said he had his "Aha" moment while listening to a presentation on memory given by neuropsychiatrist and Nobel Prize winner Eric Kandel. As Nader explained in his 2012 TED Talk, "I realized the process of remembering something causes a memory to be unstored and it has to be restored. If you could block the protein synthesis required to restore the memory, you change the memory. . . It's like rewiring the brain."

When Nader, Schafe, and LeDoux (2000) published a paper that proposed a consolidated memory could be reconsolidated, memory researchers protested. But 15 years and 300 studies later, memory reconsolidation has become a well-supported construct among brain scientists and memory researchers alike. Initially, Nader and his team experimented with rats by conditioning the sound of a tone with a shock to the rat's foot until the rat demonstrated a fear response to the sound of the tone. The next day, the researchers reexposed one group of rats to the tone again, then injected a chemical compound into each rat's amygdala that interfered with the protein synthesis required to lock the fear response in place. As a result, these rats no longer demonstrated a fear response to the sound. Moreover, this group of rats did not demonstrate spontaneous recovery of the fear as sometimes happens with traditional extinction therapy.

THE MEMORY RECONSOLIDATION TIME WINDOW

In the same study, researchers isolated a second group of rats that received the tone/shock conditioning but did not get an injection of the chemical compound until 6 hours after being reexposed to the sound. When tested later, these rats still registered a fear response at the sound of the tone.

Thus, researchers concluded that although you can change a memory after you reactivate it, you have to insert new learning within 5 hours. Otherwise, the memory reconsolidation window closes.

Subsequently, other researchers began investigating nonpharmacological interventions that could decondition a fear response permanently in humans (Agren et al., 2012; Monfils, et al., 2009; Oyarzun et al., 2012; Schiller et al., 2010). These studies also found that for successful extinction to take place, the person has to briefly reactivate the fear memory that conditioned the response, wait several minutes, then continue the extinction training within 5 hours before the memory reconsolidation window closes.

However, additional research revealed that reactivating the fear memory wasn't sufficient to open the memory reconsolidation window. For instance, Pedriera et al. (2004) and Sevenster et al. (2012) demonstrated that upon reactivation of an emotional memory, a discrepancy from what the animal or person expects must occur. Scientists call this a "prediction error" or a "mismatch" experience. Neuroscientists believe that when this prediction error gets triggered, the memory trace destabilizes and the synapses reorganize to integrate new learning into the original pathway.

How is this different from traditional extinction therapy? First, researchers have demonstrated that reconsolidation and extinction are coded in the brain differently (Duvarci, Mamou, & Nader, 2006; Suzuki et al., 2004). Extinction seems to suppress a learned fear, but it doesn't convince the mind that the aversive stimulus won't show up again. In addition, Gershman, Jones, Norman, Monfils, and Niv (2013) theorize that our emotional brains operate like one big statistical prediction machine that doesn't just learn from association, but thinks in terms of probabilities based on past experience. When the prediction error only happens during one trial or is too divergent from what the animal expects, these researchers theorize that the animal believes there is a new *latent cause* for the different outcome. Thus, the new experience gets coded as a separate learning that competes with the original learning.

For example, if you had a fear of dogs because a big, black dog bit your leg when you were a child, then you might attempt extinction by gradually exposing yourself to safe, positive experiences with dogs. Even if you begin to feel more comfortable around most dogs, you might still feel apprehensive around big, black dogs. This is because your mind infers there is some other latent cause that explains why these other dogs haven't bitten you, but it isn't fully convinced a big, black dog won't attack you again at some point.

Rather than removing aversive stimuli abruptly as is done with traditional extinction, Gershman et al. (2013) theorize that if the prediction error is presented in gradual increments, the person is more likely to believe that the *original* latent cause has been reversed. Using the previous example, say you're telling the story about being bitten by the black dog at a family reunion. In the middle of recounting your story, your mother says, "Oh honey, the reason that dog bit you is because you accidentally stepped on its tail. It had been abused before the Smiths adopted it, so he was quick to react if he thought somebody was trying to hurt him. I thought you realized that." In this example, the prediction error is not the sudden experience of a black dog being friendly, but a new contextual detail that modifies the original learning while the memory is being recalled

In addition, another group of neuroscientists from the Massachusetts Institute of Technology (MIT) were studying how the brain links the context of a memory to a particular emotion. Redondo et al. (2014) identified a specific neuronal circuit that connects the amygdala (which tags the emotion) to the hippocampus (which provides the context). In one study, the researchers were able to diminish the association of fear with a memory in mice by simultaneously reactivating the fear memory while presenting the mice with a rewarding experience. Moreover, the scientists found new connections were made between the hippocampus and amygdala that weakened the fear response and strengthened positive associations with the memory's environmental cues. Infusing positive experiences that change the memory of an unpleasant experience is what I learned to do in Rapid Resolution Therapy. Similarly, Ecker, Ticic, and

Hulley (2012) describe it as juxtaposing a mismatch experience with the earlier memory.

THE MISMATCH EXPERIENCE

While researching and developing their coherence therapy model, Ecker and Hulley observed transformative change occurred when the client held awareness of an earlier emotional event (and the learning associated with it), while simultaneously experiencing an updated perspective that contradicted or disconfirmed the original learning. Naturally, these clinicians were delighted when the memory reconsolidation research began to support what they had been observing for over 20 years. As a result, Ecker, Ticic, and Hulley wrote *Unlocking the Emotional Brain* (2012), the first clinical text to translate the applications of memory reconsolidation research for psychotherapy.

Inferring from the theory proposed by Gershman et al. (2013), the mismatch experience must broaden and update the client's perspectives regarding the *latent cause* of an event. For example, in the last chapter I talked about my client Ian who attached the emotional meaning "*Don't believe in anything*" to the experience of his father leaving. In order to change this belief, he recalled the memory of the day his dad left, then contrasted it against recent experiences that invalidated these earlier beliefs.

One of the experiences that accomplished this for Ian was recalling two recent encounters where he played music with a group of friends in front of a small crowd. As he imaged this, I encouraged him to immerse himself in the rhythm of the music and notice what he sensed from his fellow musicians and the crowd as he played. Ian said, "I feel connected to them. Like they are glad I am there . . . Like my music means something to them . . . Like they believe in me." He also recalled that he enjoyed talking with a few people after these particular performances without feeling so anxious.

With this contrasting experience in mind, I asked Ian to return to the memory of his father leaving home and describe it without emotionally reliving it. Ian was able to chronicle the event with much less distress this time. When he got to the part of the story where his father left without hugging him or saying "goodbye," Ian retorted, "I see it now. My dad was alcoholic and socially awkward and pretty much kept to himself all the time. He was that way with everybody. It wasn't just me."

Ian continued, "As I reflect on it now, maybe he left without talking to me or hugging me because he couldn't deal with being close to people or handling emotions. I don't think he could bear to see my pain. He didn't know how to deal with it." In addition, Ian contrasted this earlier memory with present-day interactions with his father. His dad had been calling him recently and seemed to be attempting to have a relationship with Ian, but their phone conversations were short and awkward. Though Ian still felt frustrated with his dad's inept social skills, he realized his dad seemed to care about their relationship.

CORRECTIVE EMOTIONAL EXPERIENCES

As I was describing the concept of mismatch experiences, you may have been thinking, "Isn't this what we used to call a corrective emotional experience?" The answer is, "Yes." However, to be effective, the corrective emotional experience has to be contrasted simultaneously with the old emotional learning.

Corrective emotional experience research dates back to the 1940s, when psychoanalysts Alexander and French (1946) attempted to determine what conditions create therapeutic breakthroughs. Interestingly, Sharpless and Barber (2012) noted that Alexander and French concluded that for transformation to occur the client had to be reexposed to the memory of an earlier traumatic experience while having someone he trusts react to him with a completely different attitude from the original persons involved in the event. Or the client would have to stumble upon something novel as he encountered an event similar to the original trauma that would change its context. Although Alexander and French focused more on the therapeutic conditions that produce a corrective experience, it is interesting that they also acknowledged the therapist had to implement the corrective emotional experience while juxtaposing the client's prior experience of the traumatic event.

Ecker et al. (2012) opine that because the memory reconsolidation erasure process is a neurological construct, it is not limited to any single psychotherapy model. The authors believe that as long as therapists follow the transformation sequence of "Reactivating, mismatching, and revising with new learning," they are free to use their choice of experiential techniques to carry out the process.

In addition to Ecker and Hulley's coherence therapy model, other therapy approaches that appear to follow this transformation sequence include EMDR, accelerated experiential dynamic psychotherapy, interpersonal neurobiology, emotion-focused therapy, somatic experiencing, sensorimotor therapy, holographic reprocessing, and Rapid Resolution Therapy (RRT).

THE RECON PROCESS

With this in mind, I developed a protocol that I use called the RECON process that combines the best of what I think all of these therapy approaches have to offer, while keeping the procedure flexible enough for you to adapt to your own theoretical background and skills. My training in Connelly's (2014) RRT model inspired the RECON process. However, the RECON process also integrates what I've learned from other trauma-therapy models, the memory reconsolidation research, and most important, my clients. For example, the RECON process utilizes the Affect Bridge technique to locate a pertinent memory, which is similar to EMDR's floatback technique and interpersonal neurobiology's affect scan. In addition, the RECON process allows for inclusion of techniques I've learned in coherence therapy that assist the client in uncovering "pro-symptom positions" that have kept an implicit schema in place. Yet the way I create mismatch experiences has been influenced by Connelly, who has crafted ingenious ways of triggering positive mismatch experiences that utilize hypnosis, imagery, stories, humor, and role play. I'll get into more of these creative interventions in Part III of this book.

I use the acronym RECON to outline my therapeutic reconsolidation process:

1. **R**ecall the current undesired emotional response *briefly*.
2. **E**xplore for a similar emotional memory and the associated beliefs and behaviors that got attached to the event.
3. **C**reate a calm, positive experience that elicits the desired response.
4. **O**bservationally describe the troubling memory while remaining emotionally present.
5. **N**eutralize negative emotional meanings with contrasting positive experiences that update the original learning.

In the paragraphs that follow, I'll illustrate how to use the RECON process through a case example. The case involves my client Carol, a 34-year-old mother who obsessively worried about her son Nate going near large bodies of water since he was a baby. When Nate was 11 years old, Carol reluctantly let him take swimming lessons. To her relief, he actually swam very well in a supervised pool, but that didn't assuage her fears. At the time of our meeting, Nate had just turned 14 years old and wanted to attend a school field trip to the beach. At first Carol refused and Nate became enraged. He told her he was tired of her overprotectiveness, and they argued bitterly about it for days.

Carol realized that her fears were irrational and contacted me for therapy. In the first session, we built rapport and identified the ideal image of what she desired. We used the second session to explore any past memories or embodied beliefs that could be driving the obsessive fear of her son going near water. Next I go through each of the steps of the RECON process that we used in this session.

STEP 1:
Recall the current undesired emotional response briefly.

To start the process, I asked Carol to bring up the intense fear she felt at the thought of her son away on a trip, swimming in the ocean. Within moments her face turned pale and she put her hands on her abdomen as she said, "I feel panicky, like my insides are quivering." I asked Carol if she could describe where she felt the quivering in her body more specifically, gently noticing the sensations without judging them. Here is how the rest of the conversation unfolded:

Carol: My legs are shaking and I feel a churning in my stomach.
Therapist: Okay. What thoughts come up with those sensations?
Carol: He's going to die and I can't stop it from happening. But, if I stop him from going, he'll hate me. I know that sounds extreme, but that's what I feel.
Therapist: I understand. That's how it's been feeling. Let's pause and take a few deep breaths as you get reoriented here. Tell me something about Nate that's interesting or funny.
Carol: [Smiling] He's smart and he's athletic. He hangs out with nice kids and has no interest in hanging out with kids who drink or do drugs. He'd rather be playing soccer and doesn't want to do anything that would harm his body.

Step 1 Commentary: The first step of the process is to have the client get in touch with the undesired feeling briefly, just enough for her to map out the sensations and thoughts associated with the current undesired response. Recollecting the feeling for a couple of minutes is sufficient. You want the client to bring enough of the sensations to elucidate associated implicit learnings, but you don't want the client's sympathetic nervous system to become hyperaroused. Not only is sympathetic hyperarousal unpleasant, but it can also inhibit hippocampal processing, which prevents the memory from getting adaptively integrated into explicit memory. To prevent Carol's nervous system from becoming hyperaroused, I redirected her to pause, breathe, and shift her attention to something pleasant (sharing positive qualities about her son).

STEP 2:
Explore for a similar emotional memory and the associated beliefs and behaviors that got attached to it.

Once I saw that Carol had returned to a calmer state, I asked her to turn on a little bit of the panicky feeling again and follow the sensations in her stomach and legs back to an earlier time she could remember having similar feelings. I asked her to let me know at any time if it felt too intense and we could pause and stop the process. I reassured her this was not meant to be painful, and encouraged her to be patient with herself as she explored any sensations, images, feelings, or thoughts that came to mind.

She held her eyes closed for several minutes, and then she said, "It's not totally clear yet, but it seems like I'm remembering a time at the beach with my parents. I was 6 years old, I think." Carol sat quietly for another minute, and then opened her eyes wide exclaiming, "Oh my God, that was the time my mom almost drowned in the ocean. I cannot believe that I never made that connection."

"Mm-hmm," I said encouragingly. "I want to hear more about that incident, but first let's do something that will make it easier for you to tell me that story."

Step 2 Commentary: As illustrated in this example, tracing the physical sensations back to a time the client can remember having a similar feeling usually leads to a relevant memory. At this stage, you only need the client to briefly describe the emotional memory. As I mentioned in Step 1, the client does not need to get into great detail or emotionally relive the event because this could overactivate the sympathetic nervous system. Tell the client all you need is one sentence that describes the gist of the event such as "My *step-father molested me . . .* My *mom went to the hospital . . . etc.*" This brief description is enough to unstore the emotional memory and start the memory reconsolidation time clock ticking. You can also use the worksheet for Locating an Embodied Belief that I provided in Chapter 4 for this part of the process.

If the client says she can't find a salient memory connected to the body sensations, ask her to scan through a few major events in her life and select one that seems the most relevant or disturbing. Although this approach may not pinpoint the exact implicit memory, the client is likely to get into the ballpark of an associated event. On the other hand, if the client identifies several related memories, ask her to select the one that seems the most troubling or representative of the pattern. It's best to only work with one memory at a time.

STEP 3:
Create a calming, positive experience that elicits the desired response.

Before going into further detail about the traumatic memory, I collaborated with Carol to create an experience of the emotional response she desires. This goes back to a few of the concepts I discussed in Chapter 2: Eliciting Exciting Goals. Often, the therapist will have to initiate a suggestion because the client is too close to the problem and may not be able to conceive of an alternative way of feeling and thinking yet.

Therapist: I wonder if you can see letting Nate go on this beach trip as a positive milestone for you both, kind of like other milestones such as when you dropped him off at school the first time, let him dress himself, play soccer, take swim lessons, and other new experiences that you both successfully navigated. I know milestones can be bittersweet because you realize he's growing up and he's not a baby anymore. But imagine picking him up from school after this trip, and seeing that big grin on his face, with all these great stories to tell you, and you two feeling even closer because you let him go.

Carol: I like that. That's a good focus point. Thinking of me picking him up from school and seeing him happy feels good.

Therapist: Great. Anything you want to add or change about that image?

Carol: No, that's a really good thing for me to focus on. When I think about that, I feel a sigh of relief and warmth in my heart.

Therapist: Okay, close your eyes and imagine him getting off the bus, smiling . . . he runs up to you excited and can't wait to tell you about everything . . . you can tell he's so glad you let him go on this trip . . . You may even sense that he missed you a little bit, too. Now imagine long threads like thin silver cords connecting you so you can talk to him in your mind whenever you like and send him love, light, and protection. Sense how you're always connected, even when you're not physically present in the same room. Send him love right now and hear what he might say back to you, knowing he loves you and wants you to be okay. Then whenever you're ready, find your way back here and open your eyes.

Carol: [Lightly wiping her eyes] That was cool. I imagined talking to him and letting him know I loved him and heard him say back to me, "You've showed me the right way, Mom. Now let me go and let me grow!" I feel better already.

Step 3 Commentary: My training in RRT and hypnosis taught me to create a calm, positive experience by connecting the client to a multisensory image of what is desired before reviewing any traumatic material in detail. Imagery works better than just identifying positive thoughts because imagery engages the emotional brain more fully.

Other trauma therapy approaches use "safe-place" imagery or teach clients emotional regulation strategies such as mindfulness and breathing techniques that can work for this part of the process, too. Yet I like having the client imagine the response that is desired because it begins to introduce new ways of perceiving the situation at both implicit and explicit levels. Furthermore, imagining the desired future instills hope and begins to set up the mismatch experience required for memory reconsolidation.

RRT describes this technique as creating a "Future Model." Similarly, Bill O'Hanlon (2011) calls this technique a "future pull," likening it to the visualization coping skills Victor Frankl used to survive the concentration camps during the Holocaust.

STEP 4:
Observationally describe the memory while remaining emotionally present.

Now that Carol was feeling more calm and hopeful, she was in a better position to review the traumatic emotional memory. I instructed Carol to describe the details of what happened the day her mom almost drowned, but to tell it like she was observing it. I emphasized that I did not want her to emotionally relive the event, but to stay "emotionally present," as we say in RRT. Siegel (2010b) refers to this as "dual awareness" of past and present and believes it initiates reprocessing of the event through the hippocampus into explicit memory.

Carol: I was 6 years old playing in the sand next to my daddy on the beach while my mom was relaxing out on a yellow banana float in the ocean. I was only paying attention here and there when suddenly my dad started running really fast toward the ocean. Then I saw him pull her out of the ocean and walk her back to the shore. She was coughing and gagging and crying. He had his arm around her, and a few people gathered around to make sure she was okay. Then, I ran down to where they were. Mom looked scared and was crying, which made me cry. I asked her what happened and she said that she got pulled under by the tide and couldn't get back up. We went back to our towels and sat out there for a while so she could catch her breath, then we walked back to our hotel room.

Therapist: Okay, so that was a scary moment for you and your family, and *it's good your mom pulled through that.* Tell me about a better moment that happened later with you and your mom, whether it was something else you experienced during that same vacation or later in your life where you two were having a good time. Our minds have a tendency to stop the movie in the worst place, so let's finish the story at a better place to change the context of the memory.

Carol: Well, we actually went swimming in the pool the next day and my mom was fine. She played with me in the pool and then we went shopping. She bought me a new outfit from the surf store and then we went to eat at a nice restaurant.

Step 4 Commentary: The emotional brain confuses what is imagined with what is real, so if the client tells the story as if it is happening again, it can cause the emotional brain to trigger the fight-flight-or-freeze response thinking it needs to prepare the client to deal with danger. As stated earlier, this has the effect of knocking the hippocampus and prefrontal cortex offline, which are the areas of the brain that need to be online to put the memory into current context (van der Kolk, 2006).

You assist the client in remaining emotionally present by first instructing her to intend to stay present as she's retelling the story. Let her know it's okay to take breaks and pause if she finds herself reliving the incident. In addition, the therapist should pay attention to the client's level of arousal by observing the client's body language, facial expressions, and physiological responses. If you see the client show signs of autonomic arousal like sweating, shaking, dissociating, turning pale, or flushing, then simply ask her to pause and do something that gets her back into connection with you in the present moment. For example, you can say, "You're telling the story well, but it looks like you may be reliving it. Take a breath and get back here with me for a moment." Usually that is enough to prompt the client to reorient to the present moment and realize the difference between telling the story and reliving it.

You can also ask the client to name things she can see or hear in the room, take calming breaths, or recall her ideal image. You could even say something funny to the client that breaks the tension. For example, one of my colleagues who works with military veterans will ask the client a completely unrelated question like "Hey, you're doing a good job telling the story, but you're reliving it too much. Get back here and let's talk about something else for a minute like . . . what's your favorite breakfast cereal?" On paper that statement might sound insensitive, but it actually causes most clients to laugh and realize the therapist is just trying to help them relax.

Describing the event while remaining emotionally present also can serve as a type of mismatch experience for the client because he or she is recounting the story without all the emotion that was attached to it previously. I believe this helps the emotional brain separate the data about the event from the emotional meaning that was attached. As the client is retelling the story, you want to listen for distorted meanings and embodied beliefs her mind has been attaching to the event. Then you'll assist the client in experientially neutralizing those meanings in Step 5 as described next.

STEP 5:
Neutralize negative meanings with contrasting positive experiences that update the original learning.

The last step of the RECON process is to neutralize distorted meanings that got attached to the event by contrasting positive experiences that invalidate the original learning. One way to do this is to explain to the client that you are going to repeat the story back to her while purposely including errors and asking her to correct you. This strategy serves a few purposes. First, it gets the client focused on the facts of the story rather than staying stuck in the emotion around it. Second, it provides a way for the therapist to purposely exaggerate distorted meanings the client's mind associated with the event so the client can recognize the distortions and correct them. Third, the therapist can subtly suggest new meanings that the client can begin to integrate into her story. Here is how I retold the story with errors to Carol and asked her to correct me.

Therapist: You were 56 years old.
Carol: [Laughs] No, I was 6 years old.
Therapist: Right, you were 6 years old. You were playing in the sand at the beach next to your dad when suddenly he took off running toward the ocean. He saw that your mom had gotten pulled under the water

due to the rip current. He was able to get her above water, but he had to drag her to the shore and perform CPR on her.

Carol: No. He didn't have to do CPR. He pulled her out of the water, put his arm around her, and walked her to the shore. She gagged and coughed up the water.

Therapist: A lifeguard showed up and he looked like David Hasselhoff.

Carol: [Laughs] No! A few people showed up to help, but she was doing okay. So we came back to our towels on the beach and rested for a while. Then we went to our hotel room.

Therapist: As soon as you got to the hotel room, she threw the banana float in the trash can and swore she would never go back into the ocean.

Carol: No, she kept the float and she still goes into the ocean. She didn't let that stop her. She learned that if you get caught in a rip tide, you turn your body so it is parallel to the beach. Toes and nose, as they say. We taught Nate this, too, so he knows what to do.

Therapist: That's smart. Your mom learned what to do, taught you and Nate how to do it, and feels okay going back into the ocean now.

Carol: Yeah, she's fine. Gosh, I've been holding Nate back from getting in the ocean because of that suppressed fear. But he knows something that she didn't know then. He's not going to be reckless, or be out there by himself on a float, or be out there at night. I can think about it more rationally now.

Therapist: Great. Run the memory back through your mind and tell me how it *feels* now.

Carol: [Closes her eyes for a moment] Wow. That's amazing. It feels so much different now. I see the scene, but I can see now that my mom panicked then because she didn't know how to react to the situation. She knows what to do now and hasn't let that event stop her from going in the ocean. She taught me to get your body parallel to the beach and if you act calmly you can get yourself out of trouble and we've taught Nate that.

Therapist: Yes, your mom figured it out and taught you and Nate what to do.

Carol: Yeah. That's amazing. I can't believe how just rewiring that one little memory has made me feel totally different about this situation. I feel like I can be much more rational about it now.

Step 5 Commentary: This error-filled retelling approach is another strategy I learned from RRT. I like to use this technique because it is collaborative and it begins to elucidate distorted meanings for the client right away. When retelling the story back to the client, take on the role of a "dumb detective" and let the client initiate changing the meaning by correcting you. If you make interpretations or directly suggest how to change the meaning of the past event, it will not be nearly as effective. The goal is to throw errors in the story that get the client questioning prior meanings and updating the story's context herself.

For Carol, I exaggerated the story by saying her mom needed CPR and swore she'd never go in the ocean so that Carol was in the position of *convincing me* that her mom was okay. Similarly, infusing absurd humor helps decrease anxiety and forces the client to make a more coherent narrative out of the implicit memory. Most clients enjoy the humorous elements, but use your clinical judgment. You don't want the client to feel like you are minimizing her experience. Carol's specific phobia responded very well to this intervention. But clients with more complex trauma may need additional rounds of the RECON process with several related memories.

To sum up, neuroscience research now validates that you can change prior emotional learning at its source, but you have to follow the conditions required for memory reconsolidation. Those conditions include the following: (1) reactivating the original memory; (2) producing a prediction error or mismatch experience; and (3) presenting or repeating new learning within 5 hours, before the memory reconsolidation window closes.

To translate these conditions for the therapy room, you can use what I call the RECON process. The RECON process combines the best elements of what I think modern therapy approaches offer, while being simple enough for you to adapt to your practice setting and therapy style.

Worksheet 5.1 presents a RECON worksheet you can use as a quick guide in your sessions. Of course, the real trick lies in Steps 3 and 5 of the RECON process—creating positive experiences that elicit the desired emotional response and neutralizing negative meanings. The next section of this book provides a plethora of experiential strategies you can use for either of these two steps that draw from imagery, storytelling, play, humor, music, and movement. You'll also learn how these creative techniques positively engage the emotional brain, so that change occurs at both conscious and unconscious levels.

WORKSHEET 5.1: RECON Process

1. **R**ecall the current undesired emotional response *briefly*.

2. **E**xplore for a similar emotional memory and the associated beliefs and behaviors that got attached to it. (Use the Locating Embodied Beliefs worksheet in Chapter 4.)

3. **C**reate a calm, positive experience that elicits the desired response.

4. **O**bservationally describe the memory while remaining emotionally present.

5. **N**eutralize negative emotional meanings with contrasting positive experiences that update the original learning.

PART III

ACTIVATING EXPERIENTIAL CHANGE

CHAPTER 6

Invoking Inspirational Imagery

Research suggests the brain responds to an imagined experience almost as much as it does to a live encounter. This is why we emotionally react to dreams, literature, movies, theater, and even video games. Similarly, you can dramatically change the way a client feels about a situation, relationship, and her identity by invoking an imagined experience in a session. This chapter will give you several ideas for invoking imagery that you can use for reconsolidating a memory using the RECON process. For example, imagery can be used for Step 3 (*Create a calming, positive experience that elicits the desired response*) or Step 5 (*Neutralize negative meanings with contrasting positive experiences that update the original learning*).

SCIENTIFIC SUPPORT FOR GUIDED IMAGERY

The use of imagery in psychotherapy dates back to the late 19th century when both Janet and Freud used imagery as a tool to assist patients in resolving traumatic memories. Janet recognized that intrusive images of traumatic events were a primary source of distress and assisted his patients in replacing troublesome mental pictures with neutral or positive images. Freud viewed images from dreams as a rich source of unconscious material and also explored imagery that arose for the patient during free association. (Hackmann, Bennett-Levy, & Holmes, 2011). Jung also regularly encouraged imagery through use of what he termed "active imagination." Moreover, humanistic therapy pioneers such as Fromm, Perls, and Gendlin advocated working through issues using imagery.

Even the cognitive-behavioral tradition of psychotherapy embraced imagery as a powerful resource. In fact, as early as 1971, Aaron Beck proposed the brain had two systems for processing information—one system being more verbal and rational, and another system that was nonverbal and processed stimuli in a more immediate, sensory way. Subsequently, cognitive-behavioral researchers such as Foa, Steketee, Turner, and Fischer (1980); Dadds, Bovbjerg, Redd, and Cutmore (1997); and Arntz, Tiesema, and Kindt (2007) found that substituting imagery worked just as well as live events when setting up exposure interventions, classical conditioning trials, and systematic desensitization. Guided imagery even produces physiological changes in the body. For instance, McKinney et al. (1997) showed that guided imagery with music reduced symptoms of depression and lowered cortisol levels within 6 weeks for a group of participants who reported symptoms of mild to moderate depression prior to the study.

As psychotherapy adopted the use of imagery as a therapeutic tool, the practice of medicine began incorporating it, too. A profusion of research in the 1980s and 1990s supported guided imagery's role in relieving pain, accelerating recovery from surgery, enhancing immune function, lowering blood pressure, and even in reducing cholesterol (Achterberg, 1986; Naparstek, 2004; Rossman, 2010; Sheikh, 2002).

IMAGERY AND THE BRAIN

Early guided imagery experts hypothesized that imagery worked by activating right hemispheric processing in the brain, but in actuality, both the left and right hemispheres are involved in producing and processing imagery experiences. Farah (1988) proposed that mental imagery is actually a function of the visual system in the brain, which represents information in the form of retinotopical maps that are connected to our emotional centers.

Harvard researcher Stephen Kosslyn (2005) agreed with Farah's observations and followed with extensive study on how the visual centers of the brain process mental imagery. He found that two thirds of the areas of the brain that are involved in visual perception of actual physical objects are also activated when we merely imagine the object. A study by Kreiman et al. (2000) also identified common neural substrates for the processing of incoming visual information and recalling visual images from memory. When we physically look at something, the raw data of the object's properties hit our retina, much like a cluster of pixels we see in a computerized image. The brain then compares this raw information to prior mental maps of images and interprets what the current image is based on our prior experiences.

Likewise, when we recall or imagine a scene, our emotional centers respond to activation of visual stimuli and react as if the event is happening in real time. Granted, the intensity of an imagined scene may not be as robust as experiencing a live event, but it is often tangible enough to elicit an emotional and physiological response.

CRAFTING MEANINGFUL IMAGERY EXPERIENCES

Although the term "imagery" implies visualization, imagery actually refers to a mental representation that involves any or all of the senses, including sight, sound, smell, taste, and touch. For instance, a person who wants to imagine a scene to induce relaxation might not be able to "see" an image of his favorite beach, but he might feel relaxed upon recalling the sounds of the ocean waves, the feel of the sand on his feet, or the smell of the salty sea air. Although 55% of the population reports the ability to "visualize," some clients will insist they can't visualize. For these clients, explain that a mental image is not necessarily a clear visual picture of something, but more of a sensory impression of something that could involve all the senses. Studies have found that even people who have been blind since birth have the ability to evoke an internal imagery experience (Bertolo, 2005). You can build the client's confidence in his ability to use imagery by asking him to tell you the number of doors or windows in his home. Most people have to form a mental image of their home to answer that question.

Neurolinguistic programing (NLP) is a therapeutic approach that suggests clinicians assess the client's preferred sensory modality, such as visual, auditory, or kinesthetic, and craft interventions that utilize the client's preferred sense for maximal effect (Bandler, Grinder, & Andreas, 1979). To determine the client's preferred sensory modality, simply ask her to describe a beautiful scene and note whether she describes it in terms of mostly visual details, sounds, smells, touch, or feelings. NLP also makes great use of imagery by suggesting clients imagine undesirable images as being smaller, fuzzy, or further away, while making desirable images larger, clearer, or closer.

Another trick to creating powerful imagery experiences is to design the imagery not only around the client's sensory preferences but also around the client's symbols and metaphors. Symbolic images that emerge from the client's unconscious also provide keys to resolving his or her emotional issues. The rest of this chapter will show you how to evoke personal symbols and metaphors from the client and provide suggestions for how to work with the client's imagery to change the meaning of past events, inspire solutions to current problems, and facilitate healing.

EVOKING THE CLIENT'S IDEAL IMAGE

In Chapter 3, Eliciting Exciting Goals, I discussed the value of creating a sensory representation of a goal to inspire the client and kindle intrinsic motivation. You begin by collaborating with the client to develop a mental image of his or her desired response. In RRT, this is called a Future Model. As Connelly described it, "Creating the model begins the process of separating what was happening to what is now intended. With RRT, the practitioner takes responsibility for creating the model, but then checks to make sure that [the model] has the client's approval and is not conflictual" (2014, p. 7).

In RRT, the therapist initiates the description of the model because the client is often too close to the problem and can't imagine an alternative response. For example, my client Teresa from Chapter 2 who was worried about her son relapsing said she wanted to "lovingly detach" from her son, as her Al-Anon group advised. Yet she couldn't quite bring herself to do it because she had been thinking detachment meant abandoning her son. The following dialogue illustrates how I took responsibility for creating the model and better clarified the response Teresa and I intended her to have:

Therapist: So you had been thinking detachment meant distancing from Bobby, but you care about him and want to be close. Detachment actually means detaching from anything that accommodates the substance abuse. I understand you've been doing things for Bobby to avoid further complications, but you also care enough about him to let him make his own decisions and learn from his experiences.

Teresa: Yes, I realize he won't learn anything if I keep doing things for him.

Therapist: Yes. So let's create a model of you being okay letting Bobby make his own decisions, learning from both his mistakes and his successes. Can you think of an earlier time when you had to let Bobby do something on his own so he could learn how to do it and he did okay—even though you felt scared at first?

Teresa: Oh, yes! Letting him drive a car when he was a teenager.

Therapist: Well, can you imagine attempting to teach him to drive by sitting on his lap behind the wheel with your feet on his, pushing the pedals? How would that have been?

Teresa [laughing]: Right. That would have been a total mess. Even sitting in the passenger's seat barking commands would mess him up. I had to let him start out with small trips, and gave him more freedom as he demonstrated he could manage short trips and outings safely.

Therapist: Great analogy. Okay, so let's get an image of you being like that with this recent situation. I'm seeing you clear, secure, and steadfast in your resolve to let Bobby take responsibility for his recovery and learn from his experiences, knowing you've already provided him with all the resources that he needs, and spending time taking care of your own health and well-being. Would you change anything about that image or see any downside to it?

Teresa: No, I like that image. You're right. We have provided Bobby with the resources he needs for recovery. We actually paid a treatment center a huge lump sum for a policy that guarantees Bobby can go back there for treatment at any time and it's covered. My brother didn't have those resources, but Bobby does. His situation is not like my brother's.

Always invite the client to adjust the image with any other characteristics she would like. In addition, check to make sure the client doesn't see any disadvantage to cultivating the qualities of the ideal image. If she does, this is a good thing because it usually elucidates the embodied beliefs or inner conflicts that have been maintaining the client's symptoms. You can then explore and reprocess this material using the RECON process, or keep adjusting the ideal image until you and the client are in agreement with it. In this example, Teresa did not voice any conflicts with the image, so we continued as follows:

Therapist: I'm glad that image resonates with you. Now let's get a symbol that represents that ideal image because the part of the mind that controls emotion responds better to images than it does to words. Imagine something in nature or an animal in the wild that would represent your mind working this way: *clear, secure, empowered, at ease . . .*

Teresa: [smiling] I see a beautiful, strong white horse. Maybe this is my symbol for God, or it at least helps me feel like I can leave it in God's hands. Bobby has a white horse, too. The horse is carrying Bobby, so I don't have to. It feels good, like the horse will take him where he needs to go. I see that I can't steer his horse and my horse at the same time.

Next, I guided Teresa through the following process with her image to integrate it more deeply into her experiential processing system. I call this the breath-symbol induction and learned this process through my training in RRT. I demonstrate how I crafted this induction with Teresa in the next section and have included a script you can use with your clients in Worksheet 6.1 at the end of this chapter.

Breath-Symbol Induction (Adapted from Rapid Resolution Therapy)

Okay, Teresa. Imagine the white horse and take a deep breath in. That's it. Now, slowly exhale. Good job. Okay, do it again. Look up, imagine the horse again, with all it's strength and beauty, and take a deep breath. There you go, exhale and release. Okay, one more time, see the white horse, slowly breathe in, and this time rest your eyes closed as you exhale. Now with your eyes resting closed, you may or may not imagine the horse as you are aware of your breath, noticing you can breathe slower and deeper than you normally breathe . . . and as you see, hear, and sense the white horse, imagine breathing in the desirable qualities of that horse . . . graceful, powerful, secure, at ease . . . The horse just carries you and Bobby's horse carries him. It's not chasing Bobby down, it's hanging out doing what is healthy for it to do, moving ahead, leading the way . . .

Teresa stayed with this image a few more minutes, then opened her eyes and smiled. She commented, "That was neat. I had the image of riding on the horse's back and seeing Bobby getting on his own horse. But you're right; we couldn't chase Bobby down to make him get on the horse. We just had to keep doing what we knew was healthy. Bobby saw how much fun we were having and came to join us on his own."

Teresa continued to use this imagery exercise to calm her anxious feelings and reinforce her efforts to let Bobby take responsibility for his own sobriety. She said the image worked better than trying to reason through her feelings because it brought to mind a state of equanimity, peace, and trust in her own Higher Power.

REPLACING NEGATIVE IMAGERY WITH POSITIVE IMAGERY

Negative imagery is often present with a variety of psychological issues such as posttraumatic stress, obsessive-compulsive disorder, depression, and social anxiety. Whether the negative images are disturbing memory fragments from past events or dreaded fears of future events, the images themselves often trigger anxiety. Clients may attempt to suppress these negative images with distraction, avoidance, or thought stopping. But these attempts rarely work long term because our minds are wired to produce the main content of an image or thought. For example, if you say to yourself "Don't worry," the subconscious mind hears "Worry!" Test it right now. *Try not* to think about a big brown bear pedaling on a purple unicycle. That furry bruin just popped right up there, didn't he?

The mind can't erase a thought/image once it is already there, but it can replace a thought or image, especially if the subsequent thought/image is more emotionally compelling than the first. For instance, instead of thinking about the unicycling bear, how about imagining jumping Jesus on a pogo stick? Which image is more prominent now? I'd wager that it's jumping Jesus because (1) it's funnier and (2) its more emotionally laden because we're now referring to a hallowed religious icon. In a similar way, you can collaborate with the client to identify a positive emotional image to displace intrusive negative images.

My client Sophia, who survived a violent rape, used the image of an oak tree to redirect and replace intrusive flashback imagery. She came up with the image much in the same way I guided Teresa in the earlier example. We started by creating an image of how she wanted to be feeling, thinking, and responding. As we explored qualities she wanted to integrate back into her life, she identified characteristics of feeling strong, secure, grounded, and resilient. When I asked her for a symbol in nature that could represent these qualities for her, an image of an oak tree emerged in her mind. I guided her to imagine the oak tree and take several slow deep breaths, sensing those qualities already residing within her. Incidentally, Sophia was better able to calm herself using this imagery than she was using mindfulness meditation techniques. This is true for many people who've experienced trauma because mindful awareness can provoke random recall of disturbing images and sensations, while guided imagery or mantra meditations focus a person's awareness and attention on something specific.

After Sophia identified the oak tree symbol in our session, she passed a beautiful, large oak tree in a park near her home. This tree happened to be one of the few trees that survived a recent tornado in the area. Although Sophia had not consciously thought of this particular tree during our session, it was remarkably close to the image she envisioned. She said that passing by this tree each day reaffirmed the belief in her own resilience. Sophia commented, "When I tried positive self-talk, I didn't believe a word I was saying. But I could identify with the tree. I could feel it. I didn't need words. Just breathing in the image of the tree calmed and strengthened me."

RECONSTRUCTING NIGHTMARES

Some clients do not struggle with intrusive images by day as much as they do with disturbing dreams at night. Therapists often assist clients in analyzing the content of the dream to produce insight into what the dream may symbolically mean. However, I think it's more effective if you assist clients in rescripting their nightmares, suggesting that they have superpowers in their dreams and can change the dreams in any way they like. Once you determine how your client would like the dream scene to change or resolve, have the client vividly imagine the dream scene playing out the preferred way a few times during the session. Then, instruct your client to practice the preferred dream sequence a few times again before she goes to sleep. The key is for the client to mentally rehearse and visualize the new dream imagery so the revised content is integrated through the experiential system. Envisioning the new dream not only eliminates the nightmares, but it also can reveal solutions to emotional conflicts underlying the dream.

For example, in my book *Transforming Traumatic Grief* (2011), I discuss a client named Cheryl who was suffering from nightmares in which her deceased, schizophrenic mother was chasing her with knives. During Cheryl's childhood, her mother actually did chase Cheryl with a knife and attempted to stab her. Ten years later, Cheryl's mother committed suicide. Cheryl acknowledged that her dreams symbolized vacillating feelings of resentment and guilt related to the chaotic relationship she'd had with her mother. When I asked Cheryl how she would like to change the dream scene, Cheryl raised her eyebrows and replied, "Honestly? I'd like for my dream self to shoot my mom and put her out of her misery so she'll leave me alone."

Because Cheryl's mom had died from a self-inflicted gunshot wound, I did not think this ending would give Cheryl peace of mind. Nonetheless, I let Cheryl play this new dream sequence out in the session and asked her if she felt any better ending the dream this way. Cheryl replied, "Actually, at first it kind of felt good to shoot her because I'm so angry with her, but now I just feel hollow and sad."

While I acknowledged the horror Cheryl had been through with her mother, I also provided Cheryl with education about schizophrenia and suggested that when her mother was alive her spirit was getting filtered through a malfunctioning brain and body. When her mother became violent during her psychotic episodes, I suggested to Cheryl that it was quite likely her mother was trying to kill her imagined demons, not Cheryl. She could agree with this because they had enjoyed pleasant moments together when her mother was lucid.

I invited Cheryl to imagine one of the better moments with her mother and bring this into the dream scene to initiate a mismatch experience. As Cheryl imaged this, her mental picture of her mother changed. Rather than seeing her mom with large black eyes, she saw her mother's eyes return to their natural shade of blue. But she said she still saw her mother holding a knife. I suggested, "This could be because your dream mother is scared and doesn't know if you are benevolent or a demon. Whenever someone is trying to scare you, it's usually because he or she feels scared. You have the power in your imagery, Cheryl, so it doesn't matter what your mom does with the knife. If she chops your arm off, you can just grow another one. See what happens if you tell your mother that you come in peace and there is nothing to be afraid of anymore."

After Cheryl integrated these suggestions, her face softened, her shoulders relaxed, and she opened her eyes. She stated, "When I told my mom that I meant no harm and just wanted her to be at peace, she dropped the knife and hugged me. Initially, I just stood there because I didn't really feel like hugging her back. But, for the first time, I can see that she really didn't hate *me*; she hated her illness and projected that onto me through her hallucinations and delusions. She was trying to kill the schizophrenia, not me."

To note, it wasn't just reconstructing the dream imagery that was valuable to Cheryl; it was also reprocessing the *meaning* of the dream and what it symbolized that was helpful to her. Many times the client's imagery experience causes them to spontaneously change the meaning of events without much guidance from the therapist.

CHANGING SELF-CONCEPT WITH IMAGERY

Another imagery exercise that I learned in RRT is what Connelly (2014) calls "Changing Internal Geography and Perceived Identity." Connelly developed this process to assist clients who struggle with persistent negative beliefs about themselves. I referred to this exercise in the Introduction to the book under the heading "Saundra's Sunrise."

To begin, ask the client to imagine a place in nature where she has seen something that was beautiful or awe inspiring. When I asked Saundra to do this, she closed her eyes for a moment and related, "I'm seeing the sun just beginning to rise over the lake. I like it when it is still a little dark and quiet outside. The colors in the sky are kind of muted, like these sheer pink-violets and soft peachy-yellows." As Saundra described this scene, her affect softened and she relaxed back into the curve of the couch, which let me know that imagining this scene was evoking a positive affective response. Then, I asked Saundra what she was noticing within herself. Saundra sighed as she murmured, "Feelings of serenity, peace, and joy."

I replied, "I'm so glad you're getting in touch with those feelings, Saundra." Then I suggested, "Let's think about it this way for a moment. Some people might say that the sunrise dropped those feelings inside of you, but I like to think that watching that sunrise brought your awareness toward your center, where you are at peace and you do have joy. Sometimes your awareness moves away from it, like on a cloudy day. But even if you can't see it, you know the sun is still there. Only your perception has changed."

The key to this imagery exercise is to evoke a sensory experience the client has already had because it is harder to deny something she has experienced firsthand. The second part of the exercise is to artfully transition the client to the concept of thinking that the experience is not outside of her, but is reflecting who she really is inside. Adding the phrase, "Let's think about it this way for a moment . . ." decreases resistance and invites the client to just try it on for a while to see if she benefits from taking this perspective.

Next, you can suggest to your client, "Let's not just think of those qualities of serenity, peace, joy as being at your center, but as who you are—your essence. You have a body, but you're not your body. It belongs to you, but it is not who you are. You have a job; you're not a job. You have thoughts, but you're not your thoughts because your thoughts can change. You have beliefs, but you're not your beliefs because those can change. So let's think of who you are as a light of peace, excitement, and wisdom that transcends the body. That light is indestructible. Nothing can harm a beam of light. Someone could curse at a light, shoot at a light, or try to cover it up, but that light keeps on shining." When I repeated this to Saundra, tears streamed down her face as she nodded and placed her hand over her heart, stating, "That is who I think I am under all this darkness. . ."

This exercise usually elicits positive responses like Saundra's, and you can use it in Steps 3 or 5 of the RECON process. It is a wonderful piece that you can serve as a powerful mismatch experience with an event that left the client feeling ashamed, worthless, guilty, or damaged.

REPROCESSING TRAUMATIC MEMORIES WITH IMAGERY

Research by van der Kolk (2006) proposed that traumatic memories are represented more in the sensory-perceptual systems than they are in the rational verbal systems. Consequently, traumatic memories can be more effectively resolved through multisensory imagery interventions than they can through verbal discussion. A common therapeutic tool is to rescript the traumatic memory by having the client imagine herself as a resourceful adult returning to the scene to assist her younger self (Capacchione, 1991; Katz, 2005; Schwarz, 2002; Watkins, 1992).

There are variations on this theme in which the adult self may take the younger self out of the trauma scene completely and say, "You don't have to be in this situation anymore. You live with me now and I'm going to respect, protect, and nurture you." Another approach may be to have the client's adult self embrace her younger self, reassuring the child that she handled the situation well given the knowledge she had at that time. A third option may be to suggest the client can change the scenario entirely, giving permission to her younger self to say whatever it is she wanted to say to the people in the trauma scene, or imagine the adults in the trauma scene apologizing and changing their behavior. Any and all of these adaptations can work, but I like to let the client choose among various scenarios to see which one feels best to her.

As an alternative, clients can also create an image of a Compassionate Guide. The Compassionate Guide imagery can be used to rescript traumatic memories, and it serves as an internal resource the client can access to develop self-compassion in the here and now. Initially, I developed this idea from Rossman's "The Inner Advisor" imagery concept. Rossman (2000) directed patients to imagine their inner advisor as "a wise, kind being who knows you well." Patients could then ask their inner advisor questions to get clarity on an illness or situation in their life, or just receive feelings of love, warmth, and kindness through this experience.

Although Rossman's Inner Advisor concept worked with many clients, some clients would feel troubled if they didn't see a clear image of a guide. They were thinking an actual figure needed to show up in a clear form. Instead, I found it more effective if I instructed the client to intentionally create his own image of what he thought a compassionate guide would be like. To prompt the discussion, I ask if there is a child, loved one, or pet for whom the client feels compassion or a sense of unconditional love. This usually elicits the feelings that will help the client compose the image of his guide. Then, I invite the client to consider the qualities he would want a compassionate guide to have, such as wisdom, patience, kindness, understanding, strength, a sense of humor, and so on.

While doing research for this book, I also came across a British psychologist named Paul Gilbert, developer of compassionate mind training. Gilbert (2009) also has developed an imagery exercise for developing an "ideal compassionate image." He advises that the compassionate image have at least these four basic qualities: (1) a wise mind, (2) strength and fortitude, (3) great warmth and kindness, and (4) a nonjudgmental attitude. Gilbert also recommends clients make a "half-smile" as they image this guide. Intentionally smiling does have the effect of eliciting pleasant feelings and thoughts. I'll explain more about why this occurs in Chapter 10, Integrating Mindful Movement. Following is a script you can use to evoke the Compassionate Guide image.

Compassionate Guide Imagery

Take a few mindful breaths and when you are ready, make a gentle smile and imagine creating an image that can represent a warm, kind, compassionate guide you can evoke whenever you would like to access wisdom, support, or comfort. Your guide may be in human form, an animal, or ethereal. Maybe it doesn't take a clear form, but just feels like a body of light or warm energy that you can receive and take in. Whatever image comes to mind is usually perfect for you, and it can even change from time to time, depending on your wants and needs.

If you'd like for your guide to be in human form, would you like for it to be male, female, or androgynous? What facial features or clothing would you give it? How old would you like the guide to be? If you envision your guide as someone familiar like an ancestor or spiritual figure, that is fine as long as you feel a sense of total acceptance and unconditional love from this figure. Imagine your guide looking at you with soft eyes and a warm smile. If you like, the guide could hold your hand, give you a hug, or lovingly embrace you in some way. If you don't get a clear image of a guide, you could just imagine breathing in light, energy, or something else that evokes feelings of warmth, love, kindness, and acceptance. As you exhale, imagine releasing pain, troubling thoughts, or tension. If you like, you can communicate with your guide, asking for advice, insight, wisdom, or perspective. I don't know if you'll get an answer now or later, but an answer will come, and often when you least expect it.

Saundra liked the idea of imagining a compassionate guide who could serve as somewhat of an internal mother figure, since her mother had been largely unavailable. Ironically, the image that came to her mind was a jolly, plump, elderly woman. Saundra found this humorous because she struggled with anorexia and was terrified of being fat. Yet she realized she liked the idea of her guide being chubby, stating, "It makes her seem even more real, lovable, and comforting."

When I suggested Saundra could imagine taking her guide with her as she reviewed disturbing memories from her childhood, she smiled. She envisioned her guide being like a "Supernanny," kind of like Jo Frost from the *Supernanny* television show. Prior to this Saundra had actually avoided reviewing past material with me because she said she had done this with previous therapists and it only seemed to make her feel worse. Yet this time she seemed intrigued.

Saundra imagined her Supernanny assertively but compassionately stepping into a scene from her childhood when Saundra's mother had been in bed for three straight days and left Saundra to care for her siblings. Saundra remembered feeling frightened, alone, and abandoned, fearing her mother wouldn't recover. She envisioned Supernanny walking into her depressed mother's room, opening the shades, and nudging her to get up and take a shower. Then, she imagined Supernanny encouragingly assisting Saundra and her siblings in getting dressed, fed, and off to school. As Saundra contrasted this imagined scene to the remembered scene of her childhood, Saundra could see more clearly how barely functional her mother was. She began to understand that what she interpreted as cold, aloof, and critical behavior from her mother was actually withdrawal, isolation, and negative thinking caused by depression.

As Saundra continued to review these childhood scenes with Supernanny, she also realized that her mother didn't start becoming more functional until Saundra became anorexic. This insight had never presented itself before. Suddenly, Saundra realized the embodied belief driving her symptoms was, "If I am happy and healthy, my mother will die. I must suffer like she suffers."

Saundra imagined her Supernanny holding her lovingly through this realization and saying to her, "Your mom's depression is not your fault. Your well-being is separate from hers. You've given her much love. Bless her and move on. It's okay for you to be healthy and care for yourself as well as you care for your kids and your patients."

Saundra continued to use the imagery of Supernanny and the sunrise as a resource for centering, comfort, and support. She commented toward the end of our work together, "Other therapists told me I needed to learn to love myself, but you are the only one who actually *showed* me how to do that. Thank you." Saundra was right. She could have never *thought* her way into loving herself. She needed someone to show her a way to *evoke* the experience of self-compassion.

To summarize, imagery is a simple, yet powerful tool to assist clients in setting goals, changing self-image, and reprocessing traumatic material. Imagery is not just visual; it can involve all the senses, and it is a good idea to determine if your client more readily processes information visually, auditorily, or kinesthetically. Although there are premade imagery scripts you can use for ideas, it's always best to elicit and integrate the client's preferred symbols, metaphors, and language. This chapter presented exercises you can use to evoke the client's symbols and metaphors for creating an ideal image, rescripting dreams, changing perceived identity, reprocessing traumatic material, and cultivating self-compassion. In the next chapter, we'll elaborate on how to use the client's symbols and metaphors to craft compelling stories that inspire change.

WORKSHEET 6.1: Breath and Symbol Induction Script
(Adapted from Connelly's Rapid Resolution Therapy™)

Begin by collaborating with the client to create an image of his or her desired emotional response, then ask the client to imagine something in nature or an animal in the wild that represents his or her desired qualities. When you have the client's symbol and understand the attributes the client associates with it, proceed with the script below:

Rest with your eyes closed and imagine your *[name client's symbol]* as you take a deep breath in. That's it. Now slowly exhale. Good job. See that *[symbol]* again and inhale. There you go, and slowly exhale. Now, you may or may not continue imagining your *[symbol]* as you are aware of your breath, noticing you can breathe more slowly and deeply than you normally breathe . . . imagine breathing in the qualities of that *[symbol]* . . . letting the essence of that *[symbol]* infuse every cell, every tissue, every fiber of your being, as your mind sets up more and more for what is represented by *[symbol]* and your ultimate well-being.

That's it, and whenever you exhale, you release what you no longer need back into the earth, where it transforms that energy into *[name qualities of symbol]*. . . then you can imagine taking that transformed energy up from the ground through your feet . . . legs . . . hips . . . that's it . . . that energy keeps traveling through your abdomen, back . . . Yes, all the way up through your spine . . . spreading through your head, where it clears, heals, organizes, and supports all of those things that are in your best interest . . . revealing peace, light . . . wisdom. And all of that is just working for you whether *[symbol]* comes to mind or not. That's it . . . and when you're ready, ever so gently, find your way back here, and take a big breath in . . . and slowly open your eyes.

CHAPTER 7

Conjuring Up Compelling Stories

Advertisers, religious leaders, politicians, and public speakers understand the power of story to inspire, motivate, and compel a person to action. We communicate, dream, and remember in narrative. Moreover, story is the vehicle people use to deliver their difficulties to us in the consulting room. Clients don't arrive with a list of facts, figures, and neatly drawn genograms—and we might be tempted to give them a certain diagnosis if they did. Instead, they present with spellbinding dramas, fiery romances, gripping dilemmas, and intriguing mysteries, as they seek our help to connect the clues and piece their personal plots together.

As the client's story unfolds, therapists can play the role of a managing editor of sorts, assisting the client in rewriting her life story so it has more consistency, cohesiveness, and meaning. Likewise, sharing stories, parables, and myths in the consulting room is a great way to stir clients emotionally and drive home the points you want to make. In this chapter you'll get ideas for ways to help clients reconsolidate a memory through rescripting their stories with new endings and perspectives. You'll also discover the elements of a good "teaching tale" and learn how to convey metaphorical stories that compel your clients to action.

Conjuring up stories can be used in Step 3 of the RECON process to create a calm, positive experience of the response the client desires. In addition, sharing stories or assisting clients in rewriting their stories can be used for Step 5 of the RECON process. Listening to and creating narratives accesses both cortical and subcortical areas of the brain and can be a great way to neutralize negative meanings of past events and update emotional learning.

THE POWER OF PARABLE

Before the age of neuroscience, medicine men in ancient cultures actually prescribed stories for mental afflictions (Stone, 1996). Administering anecdotes laced with themes of perseverance, renewal, and resilience were believed to soothe weary souls and kindle a place within the psyche that would light the way out of darkness. Though modern medicine has evolved since then, storytelling has continued to be a mainstay across cultures. Whether it is tenderly reading bedtime stories to children at night, warmly gathering around a campfire to tell tall tales, or faithfully listening to parables passed down through generations, people rely on stories for guidance and connection. Authors and filmmakers have speculated the human predilection for storytelling must be hard-wired into our brains, and indeed, neuroscience now validates that it is.

Split-brain researcher and University of California professor Mike Gazzaniga (2002) believes the impetus to create stories is driven by the logical, verbal left hemisphere's need to interpret moods, events, and behavior. Similarly, in his book *Mindsight*, Dan Siegel (2010b) posits that story can calm emotion as we engage our left hemisphere's drive to "order the details" of the barrage of affective and sensory input emanating from our emotional brain and right hemisphere. Additionally, Siegel asserts that the ability to provide a meaningful, coherent narrative of one's life promotes good mental health. Likewise, Michael White and David Epston (1990) created narrative therapy, an effective therapeutic approach that assists clients in restorying their lives.

Packing information into a compact story is not only an efficient way of organizing the massive amounts of stimuli we encounter everyday; but stories can provide essential guidance for survival. For instance, one of Aesop's Fables literally saved the life of a client of mine during a violent rape. She was a home health physical therapist visiting an elderly male patient's home for the first time. While she was doing the intake interview, the man made several inappropriate sexual comments. Although his remarks made her uncomfortable, she brushed it off, thinking perhaps the man had early-stage dementia that was causing him to lack inhibition of his speech and impulses.

However, when she bent down to get a roll of sports tape out of her bag, the man pushed her face down to the floor and positioned himself on top of her so that she could not move. As he began ripping at her clothes, she tried to get up and begged him to stop, but this only seemed to heighten his aggressiveness. Before she resigned herself to defenseless surrender, she remembered one of Aesop's Fables that her father read to her as a child:

> *The Wind and the Sun were disputing which was the stronger. Suddenly they saw a traveler coming down the road, and the Sun said: "I see a way to decide our dispute. Whichever of us can cause the traveler to take off his cloak shall be regarded as the stronger. You begin." So the Sun retired behind a cloud, and the Wind began to blow as hard as it could upon the traveler. But the harder he blew the more closely did the traveler wrap his cloak round him, till at last the Wind had to give up in despair. Then the Sun came out and shone in all his glory upon the traveler, who soon found it too hot to walk with his cloak on.* (Aesop, 2002, p. 45)

Upon recalling this fable, my client realized she needed to use warmth rather than force to subdue her attacker. Still face down, she lifted her head and looked over her shoulder, where she could see the rapist, and said, "I'm sorry for whoever hurt you. Please let me look at you. Let me give you a hug." Her warmth completely disarmed him. He released his grip and received her embrace as she turned her body around to face him. After holding this position for a moment, she asked if she could go to the bathroom to clean up. He agreed to let her go, but insisted on standing guard outside the bathroom door. She picked her pants up off the floor and realized her cell phone was still tucked inside the front pocket. He followed her as she carried her pants and made her way toward a small, dark bathroom down the hallway. Once inside, she was able to quietly call the police on her cell phone and stall the man until they got there.

We acquire, retain, and access information more readily when it is relayed through a story. In fact, cognitive psychologist Jerome Bruner (1987) proclaims that dressing data up in a story makes the information 22 times more memorable. My undergraduate calculus professor must have known this. Although his classes were challenging, he had the highest pass rate at our university because he taught calculus through stories. My favorites were his fanciful tales about "Mr. X wanting to date Miss Y," illustrated by his use of equations to represent their hilarious relationship problems. He also taught us meaningful applications of mathematics by sharing real-world stories, such as the way calculus assisted the Red Cross in providing enough relief supplies for victims of Hurricane Hugo. Grabbing our attention with these emotion-filled narratives gave those random chalky digits on the blackboard new meaning and purpose.

Similarly, when we tell a story, we are shaping fragments of chalky data from various regions in our brains into a comprehensible account about why things happen so we can learn from our experiences and grow. When we listen to a story, our brains literally simulate the experience of the narrator, allowing us to learn from the experiences of others without having to expose ourselves to the same risks. As we imagine the sights, sounds, smells, and movements described in the narrator's story, the same areas of our sensory-motor cortexes light up as if we're experiencing the event, too (Cron, 2012).

Sharing teaching tales with your clients also creates a deeper therapeutic bond. Researchers found that when we are listening to a story, we move into a slightly altered state of consciousness, forming a special connection with the storyteller as mirror neurons in the brain of both the narrator and listener fire up synergistically. Likewise, Milton Erickson knew stories could create a hypnotic connection and often induced trance just by telling tantalizing tales.

Be forewarned—clients can also mesmerize you with their stories, so make sure you are not the one getting hypnotized! Listening empathically to clients' stories builds rapport; yet it's also valuable for therapists to consider alternative meanings in clients' stories and to assist clients in rescripting their accounts. Transforming the meaning of an experience from a whirlwind of woebegone into a tale of triumphant mastery is empowering for your clients.

RECASTING THE PAST

Assisting clients in revising their narratives requires respectful, empathic consideration. How do you recast someone's troubled past without minimizing the pain and suffering he or she has endured? You introduce the concept of rescripting the client's stories by using the Align, Lift, and Lead language patterns discussed in Chapters 2 and 3. Recall that you *align* with the client by using the "has been" tense change as you reflect your understanding of the client's difficulties. Then, you *lift* by acknowledging the client's strengths as you *lead* the client toward a more *useful* ending to his or her story.

For example, to align, lift, and lead with a client who has survived childhood abuse, you might say, *"I hear how difficult your childhood has been and it sounds like you've come through some really tough stuff. Yet I'm also noticing this incredible sense of fortitude, wisdom, and compassion you have developed in spite of it. I realize going through those experiences was not the way you wanted to develop those assets, but you got them. Maybe we could look at how you can apply those strengths to bring more peace and satisfaction into your life now."*

This empathic reflection prompts the client to consider how she could use her experience to her advantage without patronizing her with platitudes or discounting her harrowing experiences.

CREATING NEW ENDINGS TO STORIES

Stories generally have a beginning, middle, and end. But when it comes to traumatic memories, the mind tends to end the story at the worst moment or leave the story unfinished. Thus, to resolve a traumatic memory, assist the client in finishing the story at a place where he escaped, recovered, or had a more pleasant encounter later in his life. The ending of a story doesn't necessarily have to be happy, just useful. Meaningful stories don't always promise rainbows and unicorns at the end of them; but they often depict how the main characters changed for the better or acquired rare wisdom and skills. For instance, Odysseus reunites with his father and appreciates his wife more. Oz turns out to be a sham, but the Tin Man finds his heart and the Lion discovers his courage. In Yan Martel's *Life of Pi* (2003), Pi loses his family, but he strengthens his faith and resolve, leading him to create a new family. Furthermore, Martel suggests that it doesn't matter whether we believe Pi survived 227 days at sea via sheer self-determination or that a supernatural tiger assisted him. Instead, he asks, "Which story do you prefer?" This question is central in psychotherapy. After all, you and your clients could endlessly explore why events happened and perpetually ponder what it all means. But what really matters is how we assist our clients in using their stories to redefine and live their lives.

For example, a war veteran named Patrick had horrifying flashbacks reliving the day he watched an improvisational explosive device (IED) blow his commanding officer's legs clean off. Although Patrick was able to retain his own injured limbs after the bombing, he felt paralyzed by the guilt of not being able to help his commanding officer escape the explosion. As Patrick recounted the story during Step 4 of the RECON process I described in Chapter 5, I asked him to finish the story with a more positive or meaningful event that occurred after the explosion. He liked this idea and decided to end the story with the exuberant moment of reuniting with his family when he returned home.

Patrick was deeply religious, so I also asked about his spiritual beliefs regarding death and if he could believe his commanding officer was "okay" in the spiritual sense, even if his body didn't make it. Patrick shook his head and laughed as he said, "Well he didn't die! They flew him back to the States to complete physical therapy. They also crafted three different types of artificial limbs for him. He has a pair for walking, a pair for running, and a pair for playing basketball. I hear he's doing well and is pretty good at shooting layups, believe it or not."

Simultaneously stunned and amused, I said, "That's amazing, Patrick! How about finishing the story there?"

Patrick released a slow smile as he slapped his hand to his forehead and exclaimed, "Yeah! Why haven't I ever thought of finishing the story there? Gee . . . all this time I've been replaying the scene where I literally see him blown out of the Humvee and hear the awful screams. I felt so horrible because I couldn't get over to help him or call for the Medevac because I was injured, too. I thought he was going to die right there. But yeah . . . he's alive and apparently doing better than me right now. He'd give me crap if he thought I was still torn up over this. He'd tell me to move on and be happy."

I asked Patrick to retell his story with the new ending of reuniting with his family, and imagining his commanding officer competitively playing basketball with his new prosthetics. As part of Steps 4 and 5 of the RECON process, Patrick repeated this version of the story within the memory reconsolidation time window a few more times until he could tell the story without tears or shame. Consequently, his flashbacks about the incident completely stopped after this session.

METAPHORS THAT PROMPT HEALING STORIES

Metaphors can also be good for assisting clients in rewriting their stories. As discussed in Chapter 6, Invoking Inspirational Imagery, I encourage clients to come up with symbolic images and metaphors *they* find meaningful. Then, we collaborate to create a healing story from their preferred images.

For example, a client of mine named Tess was distraught with her tendency to avoid close relationships and assumed everyone was out to hurt her. Even though Tess had been physically abused throughout her childhood, she had done a lot of good work in our therapy sessions and finally found a partner who understood her. However, her fears got triggered again when he asked Tess to marry him, causing her to distance from him. His patience for her hot and cold behavior was wearing thin, so she called me for another session after he considered calling off their engagement.

Tess dismayed, "Why do I sabotage myself like this? I thought I was getting better, but now I'm afraid I haven't made any progress at all." Then, she reluctantly admitted she'd been cutting herself again as she rolled up her sleeves and showed me the red, jagged scars on the topside of her forearms.

In the past, guided imagery had helped Tess calm her emotions, avoid cutting, and get in touch with feelings of self-worth. So I asked her for a symbolic image that would represent feeling more secure and compassionate toward herself and others. Tess immediately replied, "Elephants. They are gentle, but strong, and care for members of their herd in a tender, respectful way." As I led her in a guided imagery exercise with the elephant image, I spontaneously created this story for her:

> *Once upon a time, there was an elephant named Elsie that had been captured and put in a traveling circus. Her caretakers Boo and Hiss thought providing two meals a day and a small horse trailer filled with straw were enough to adequately care for Elsie. In exchange, they expected Elsie to run in circles tethered to other elephants, stand on her hind legs wearing feathery headdresses, and trumpet her trunk on command. If Elsie protested, cried, or was simply too tired to "perform," Boo and Hiss became very angry, striking her rump with leather whips and isolating her in the tiny, dark trailer.*
>
> *Fortunately, the ringmaster fired Boo and Hiss and released Elsie to a beautiful, country farm where the people were nicer. On the farm, Elsie made friends with an old English sheepdog named Beau. They loved to run together, nap in the sun, and wade in a cool, blue pond on the property*
>
> *Although she loved Beau, sometimes he would bark at Elsie and paw at her trunk, urging her to be more happy-go-lucky like him. There was nothing wrong with Elsie; she was just doing what ele-*

phants do. Elsie couldn't behave like a sheepdog, no more than Beau could herd sheep with a low rumble the way that she could. But, whenever Elsie sensed Beau or the farmer was upset about something, she retreated to the forest and sulked obstinately for days, worrying they may turn on her like Boo and Hiss.

On one of Elsie's forest retreats, she ran into an old horned owl. The owl saw Elsie weeping and said, "Whooo made you cry?" Elsie was shocked when she realized this large, wide-eyed bird was talking to her. You have to understand that where she comes from, the only birds that could talk were parrots, and nobody ever wanted to talk to parrots because they would only mock you.

The owl hooted again, "Whooo are you hiding from?" Stunned, Elsie stammered, "Mean old Boo and Hiss. That's who!" The owl tilted his head to the side, and said, "Whooo on earth are Boo and Hiss?" Elsie whinnied, "My keepers!" The owl turned his head from side to side and said, "Well I don't know who Boo and Hiss are, but Beau and the farmer were looking for you here this morning. Is that who you call Boo and Hiss?"

Elsie sighed with relief as she realized she'd confused the past with the present again. She explained to the owl that elephants have really good memories, but sometimes their memories are so vivid that it was hard to tell the difference between a memory and a current event. For example, whenever she sensed Beau or the farmer getting upset, she felt compelled to run away lest they whip her and lock her up in a tiny horse trailer like Boo and Hiss used to do. The owl rubbed the edge of his wing on his chin as he pondered Elsie's dilemma. He asked curiously, "Well, you just made the distinction between the past and the present just now. What helped you realize the difference?"

Elsie thought a moment, then her eyes lit up as she bayed, "Your whooing!"

The owl raised his eyebrows as he echoed, "Whose who? My who?"

Elsie nodded, "Yes, when you asked 'who' I was hiding from, it reminded me of 'who' hurt me a long time ago and realize that 'who'

I have in my life now is totally different. So, the next time I feel hurt, I can ask myself: (1) who I'm being reminding of; (2) recognize the differences in 'who' is with me at this moment; and (3) remember 'who' I want to be now."

Upon offering this story to Tess during Step 3 of the RECON process, she nodded and smiled. Presenting new perspectives of her situation through a story about an elephant for whom she could feel compassion led Tess to view herself less harshly. It also led us to expand on the metaphors and consider additional ways Tess could manage her emotions and relate to others less fearfully.

Interestingly, the symbolic images in the story emerged spontaneously and weren't preplanned. When you have a good connection with your client and allow both your imaginations to instinctively reveal images and metaphors during the session, they will come. Ironically, when I've consciously tried to conjure up a clever story before a session, it rarely happens. There is something about those magical moments interacting with clients right brain to right brain that stirs the psyche and prompts the most transformative tropes. However, it is good to keep in mind the main elements of a good teaching tale as described next.

THE ELEMENTS OF A GOOD TEACHING TALE

When crafting a teaching tale, consider that every story consists of three basic elements: (1) a *problem/conflict* that needs to be solved; (2) a *plot*, the series of events that unfold as characters attempt to resolve the problem or conflict; and (3) a *resolution*, the concluding action or learned wisdom that results from how the main characters change or resolve the problem in the story.

Years ago, Joseph Campbell (1973) posited that the most powerful myths tend to follow a pattern he called the "Hero's Journey." Campbell proposed that the reason people connect so deeply with the archetype of the hero is because in some way we all feel like we are fighting an epic battle in our lives. The hero's journey often begins with the hero merrily enjoying his home and family until he receives a "Call to Adventure," which inevitably involves a challenge or threat to his homeland or identity.

The next stop on the hero's journey is often referred to as "The Initiation," and it involves a series of trials that require the hero to develop increased awareness and skills to overcome adversity and survive. Sometimes the hero meets a soul mate or spiritual adviser on his journey who assists him in discovering gifts and provides tools that will aid him on his travels. Finally, there is the "Return," where the hero goes back home with his newfound powers and wisdom. Sometimes the return is not easy as the hero struggles with how to integrate his new wisdom into his former world. In fact, there is often a character that resists or challenges the hero when he gets home. The final challenge for the hero is to become the master of two worlds, which may require the death of something in his old world in order for his new life to begin.

SUPERHERO'S JOURNEY

A more modern take on the Hero's Journey is the Superhero's Journey. Superhero comics and movies are captivating our culture right now. Perhaps it is because we are all longing to feel empowered in what feels like a chaotic, overwhelming world full of villains. The superhero idea came to me after watching a hilarious movie called *Mystery Men*, starring Ben Stiller. In the movie, a group of misfits believe they have rare superpowers that range from Ben Stiller's character "Mr. Furious," whose power is his "uncontrollable rage," to William Macy's character "The Shoveler," whose special power involves daring deftness with a spade.

In the movie, these characters search for compadres to join their crusade and host a superpower audition party where people show up with all manner of unusual skills, like the "Waffler," whose secret power involved "truth" syrup. Laughing through this scene, I realized we all have survived unique circumstances that forced us to cultivate curious powers.

Why not prompt clients to consider the "superpowers" they forged out of their personal fires? I created a Superhero's Journey template (see Worksheet 7.1 at the end of this chapter) to guide heroic discoveries in therapy sessions, and my clients have really enjoyed it.

For instance, my client Julie, who struggled with chemical sensitivities and digestive issues, really benefited from exploring her issues through a superheroine's lens. We began the exploration with my explaining that every superheroine befalls some tragedy in her life that usually has to do with her home planet being destroyed. Julie agreed that things in her home seemed okay for a while, until what felt like a metaphoric meteor crashed into the middle of her family's dining table (i.e., the revelation that her parents were getting a divorce).

In Julie's mind, the villain or archenemy in the story became her brother, who sought to resolve the conflict by acting out his anger, thwarting Julie's relationship with her mother, and causing more destruction in the family's world. Meanwhile, Julie developed the ability to detect figurative and literal toxins in the environment. It began with her detecting toxic shame and secrets poisoning the air of her family's home. Then, it evolved to where Julie actually developed an uncanny ability to detect mold in buildings and unusual chemicals in food. People teased Julie about these abilities, accusing her of being oversensitive rather than recognizing her skills could be useful. Julie herself felt ashamed of her knack for sniffing out the noxious and attempted to hide her special senses and question her own instincts.

We agreed that superheroes are often surprised and overwhelmed by their own strengths initially and fear their powers will cause more harm than good. But over time, they learn to harness and hone those skills until they can apply them with laser sharp accuracy and realize they can be used to bring more good into the world, help others, or champion a cause. Once prompted in this way, Julie thought of all kinds of ideas for using her keen senses as a source of strength and creativity. She created a blog to help people with chemical sensitivities and learned how to trust her perceptiveness and use it to improve her sense of self.

BORROWING STORIES FROM OTHER SOURCES

Although my preference is to collaborate with clients to craft their own heroic stories, you don't have to reinvent the wheel. There are several good books you can reference for ideas for teaching tales that inspire and prompt clients to view their issues in a different light. Among my favorite books for the therapeutic use of stories are Clarissa Pinkola-Estes's *Women Who Run With the Wolves* (1995); Anita Johnston's *Eating in the Light of the Moon* (2000); Burns's *101 Healing Stories* (2001); and *Friedman's Fables* (1990) by Edward Friedman.

I've also picked up teaching tales from books, movies, songs, and my mentors Bill O'Hanlon and Jon Connelly. Following is one of Connelly's humorous stories that is great to share with people struggling with self-consciousness and social anxiety. It has all the basics of a good teaching tale, including elements of surprise, humor, and transformation of the main character.

> *You know one of my friends had this problem with terrible social anxiety. She heard that facing your fears by initiating short conversations with people was one way to shake it. Understandably, she was quite nervous about doing this and asked me for some advice. I suggested she start with something benign, like saying "Good morning" to three or four people while shopping at the grocery store. My friend liked this idea and made a plan to try out this social experiment the next day.*
>
> *As she walked into the store, she nervously headed to the produce section. She was looking at citrus fruit when a young woman walked up to get a bag of grapefruit. "Good morning," my friend says. The young woman didn't even look at her. She just took her fruit and walked away.*
>
> *My friend was a little discouraged, but she decided to keep going. She headed down the cereal aisle. A middle-aged man was coming her way. As he stopped to pick up a box of Cheerios, my friend says, "Good morning." The man smiled, winked at her, and said, "Well*

. . . it's certainly a good morning now!" Although his response was more positive, my friend blushed at his flirtation and hurriedly headed toward the frozen food section.

She stood quietly deliberating over all the varieties of frozen pizza when a teenager walked in front of her and grabbed a box of thin crust, pepperoni. She swallowed hard and then blurted, "Good morning!" The kid shrugged his shoulders and said, "Good morning yourself, lady," then farted as he walked away!

My friend just rolled her eyes. That kid's smart-aleck attitude made her even more determined to get that fourth "Good morning" delivered with all the courage and pride she could muster. She marched right up behind him to the checkout counter, put her frozen veggie pizza on the counter, and cheerfully said to the clerk, "Good morning!" The clerk smiled and said, "Good morning. How nice to be greeted by a friendly face."

Later, my friend was telling me about her day and commented, "You know, I realize I didn't learn anything about myself today. I learned about four different people at four particular moments in time. I guess that's the whole point of talking to people, right? To learn something about them."

Sharing playful stories like this actually coaxes clients to try out social experiments to decrease anxiety much more than if I directly ask them to do it. When I pass this story along in Step 3 or Step 5 of the RECON process, the client will often laugh and say, "I've thought about doing something like that to overcome my fears. Maybe I'll try that this week and remember that story about your friend if people act weird!" Clients may not carry out this social experiment in a formal, structured way; but they inevitably tell me they started saying "hi" to more people, switched their focus to learning about others instead of worrying about themselves, and notice their social anxiety decreasing.

BECOMING A SPIRITED STORYTELLER

Being from Tennessee—the state that hosts the annual National Storytelling Festival—I come from a long line of outrageous storytellers. Thus, I've grown up understanding how to spin a good yarn so that it comes to life, engages the listener, and leaves an impression. As rising raconteurs know, a story has more impact if you embellish it a little and tell it as if it happened to you or someone you know. When you deliver an allegorical anecdote in a dramatic, entertaining way, you create that altered state of consciousness that connects you and the listener.

For a story to come to life, you want your listener to identify with the protagonist emotionally and be interested in riding behind the lead character's eyes as the narrative unfolds. Use descriptive language that stimulates all five senses. Studies have shown that when we hear such metaphorical language, the corresponding sensory areas in our brain light up as if we are having the experience. For example, my aunt described the kindness of my great grandmother like "a warm blanket that someone carefully spreads over you on a cool October morning." Although I never met my great grandmother, this soothing description of her makes my emotional brain want to crawl up in her lap.

Of course, you don't have to be so poetic to have an effect on your client. Just keep your intention for the story clear and add enough detail to paint a multisensory picture of the story scenes. For instance, in the elephant story, I added just enough imagery that would help Tess identify with the elephant's surroundings, contrasting the dankness of the circus trailer against the pastoral pleasantness of the farm scene. My intention was to provoke Tess's mind to distinguish metaphorical differences between her childhood and the improved circumstances in her life now.

You can also animate your stories by using different accents or dialects for the various characters. Alternate the pitch and cadence of your voice to create the mood and build interest and excitement as you work up to the climax. For example, I kept my voice soft and melodic as I described the idyllic scenes of Elsie and the sheepdog. But, when I played the owl in the story, I mimicked what an owl might do, screeching my voice, pensively raising and lowering my eyebrows, and turning my head side to side in a thoughtful way.

As you wind your way toward the end of the story, intentionally pause before the resolution so your listener eagerly anticipates the conclusion. This stimulates the SEEKING emotional system in the brain that is interested in finding solutions. Sometimes this pause prompts clients to finish the story before I can—and many times their endings are better! You might also consider finishing the story with a funny or unexpected ending. Humor, play, and novelty really grab the emotional brain and make the story's moral memorable. Again, keep in mind that a good story does not necessarily have an ending that favors the protagonist, but the conclusion should at least suggest how the main character applies the wisdom he or she acquired through the story's events.

As we close out this chapter, I'd like to share another story I heard from Connelly. This is one of my favorite tales to use with clients struggling with obsessive thoughts:

> *You know as you're talking about being up all night with those pesky thoughts, it reminds me of this lady I know who built her dream house. It wasn't a great big house or anything, but she loved the floor plan and it was just perfect for her. One day I ran into her and asked her how she was enjoying her new home. She rolled her eyes and said, "Oh, I love it, but you're never going to believe this—the city laid railroad tracks right behind it. So, I'm going to call the Mayor this week and ask him to move those tracks. I'm not getting a wink of sleep!"*
>
> *"Oh no! Is the loud noise from the train keeping you up at night?" I asked.*
>
> *"No, no," she said. "I don't mind the sound of the train, I kind of like that sound. It's these damn hobos! They're constantly jumping off the train and coming to my house. There are hundreds of them! They come by at all hours wanting food, money, a shower, or simple conversation. I'm thawing out entire turkeys each night so I can feed them all, and my water bill is out the roof! So, I'm calling the city and telling them they've got to move those tracks as soon as possible."*

"Hmm," I replied, "Why don't you just quit letting the hobos in?"

She looked at me like I was crazy and said, "Do you think that will work?"

"Of course it will work," I retorted. "Whenever they knock on your door, you just tell them you didn't order any hobos and don't open the door. If you try to ignore them, they'll just keep knocking louder. But, if you acknowledge them and politely redirect them, they'll eventually tell all their friends and stop showing up."

"Interesting," she mused. "You think that's better than getting the city to move the tracks?"

"Well of course it is!" I exclaimed. "That track has already been laid and it's unlikely it can be moved very quickly. They're kind of like the tracks in your mind that those annoying thoughts have been traveling down. The thoughts, like the hobos, may keep showing up, but you don't have to feed, bathe, and entertain them."

In sum, we are biologically wired to enjoy and learn from hearing and creating stories. Our logical brains are driven to order the multitudes of data bombarding our senses and assemble narratives to explain why things happen. Not only does assisting your client in rewriting his or her story help neutralize negative perceptions, but hearing meaningful stories also sparks insight and change. When assisting clients in revising their stories, encourage them to finish the story at a more positive place or use the hero's journey as a guide for transforming a tale of tragedy into a narrative of triumph. Better yet, I've created the Superhero's Journey template in Worksheet 7.1 that helps clients recast their past in a fun, uplifting way.

In addition, you can create stories from the client's metaphors and symbols or inspire the client by sharing teaching tales from other sources. When you share a story in a session, make it your own, and tell it in an enchanting, playful way. Recounting a story in a lighthearted way unites you and the listener and updates old learning by engaging the SEEKING and PLAY systems of the emotional brain. We'll go into more ways to facilitate change through the PLAY emotional system in the next chapter, Priming With Play and Humor.

WORKSHEET 7.1: Superhero's Journey Template

Your Superhero Name: ______________________________

Origin Story: *(Usually begins with thinking your life or homeland was okay, until something happens to alter or destroy your world as you knew it.)*

Superpower(s): *(Special sense or skill you developed out of your life circumstances.)*

Secret or Known Identity: *(Do you tell people about your special abilities or feel like you have to keep them a secret? If you keep them secret, why?)*

Sidekick(s): *(A special friend or ally, could be a person, pet, or metaphorical figure.)*

Championing Cause: *(What injustice, principle, or cause motivates you and gives you a sense of purpose?)*

Kryptonite: *(What weakens you? Hint: It usually is something that comes from your "home" planet such as guilt, resentment, substance abuse, manipulation, etc.)*

Supernatural Guide: *(A figurative or literal being in your life that imparts wisdom, support, or guidance. Could be your higher self, may not be outside of you.)*

CHAPTER 8

Priming With Play and Humor

Play has gained serious recognition as a therapeutic tool that promotes social bonding, reduces fear, and lifts mood. Moreover, humor and laughter are ardent antidotes for depression and anxiety, but many therapists avoid using humor for fear they will offend the client—or because they don't think they can pull off being funny. This chapter will discuss how play positively affects the brain and provides you with amusing interventions that diffuse resistance, empower clients, and reduce fear and anger. These playful tools are also great to use in Step 5 of the RECON process to neutralize negative emotional meanings and reinforce new learning.

PLAY FOR NEUROPLASTICITY AND SOCIAL DEVELOPMENT

As discussed in Chapter 1, neuroscientist Jaak Panksepp believes play is not a learned behavior but is actually one of the seven primary emotional systems that is hardwired into the brains of mammals and humans (Panksepp & Biven, 2012). Initially, scientists thought that the PLAY system was merely designed to motivate us to learn about the world and build skills for survival. For example, scientists speculated that predatory animals enjoyed chasing moving objects because it developed their skills for hunting. Conversely, prey animals, like deer, were presumed to play by running, hiding, and dodging because it builds their acumen for escaping predators. Yet, as scientists dove deeper into the PLAY system, they realized that people and animals also play as a means of social connection and for the mere pleasure of goofing around.

Neurochemically, playful activity stimulates dopaminergic pathways in the reward centers of the brain and is associated with the release of endogenous opioids and cannabinoids that reduce pain and make us feel good. Furthermore, play and humor often generate creative solutions to problems and have been associated with generating "Aha!" moments of insight. For example, in a 2009 study, Subramaniam et al. demonstrated that people were better able to solve problems and puzzles when they were shown a comedy video beforehand, as opposed to watching a neutral or anxiety-provoking film before tackling a complex conundrum. Many large companies such as Google and Turner Broadcasting actually have recreation rooms and encourage employees to take "play breaks" because they know massaging the mind with laughter and games stimulates creative breakthroughs and fosters team cohesion.

In fact, play promotes positive social bonding, collaboration, and flexibility in both humans and animals. In his lab at Washington State University, Panskepp & Burgdorf (2003) and colleagues discovered mice were more responsive to researchers who tickled or played with them than they were to researchers who didn't initiate jocular gestures. Furthermore, the researchers discovered the mice made a distinct chirping sound when they were tickled or played together. When scientists amplified the volume on a recording of this chirping noise, they realized it was laughter!

You don't have to literally tickle your clients to get them in the playful spirit, but tickling their funny bone by incorporating good-natured wit and play is a great way to build rapport and activate the brain's own fix for a foul mood.

USING PLAY TO DECREASE RESISTANCE

Lighthearted play is especially useful with guarded clients who equate emotional openness with painful vulnerability. I learned this early in my career working with inner-city adolescents and the elderly. Neither of these groups was comfortable with the idea of psychotherapy, but when I started tossing a ball around or challenging them to a dance contest, they opened up and started talking.

In spite of my positive experiences using play in groups, I was hesitant about being playful in individual sessions because I feared the client would think I was not taking his issues seriously. When I took the risk with a few stuck clients, however, I was surprised to find they were very receptive to using play to work through difficult emotions.

Being silly helped create a sense of safety, especially with clients like Michael, who liked to spar and use sarcasm as a defense. We'd been working together for months on his struggles with alcoholism and a debilitating phobia of driving over bridges. Unfortunately, this bridge phobia severely limited his world, since our town is nicknamed Bridge City, and you can hardly go anywhere without driving over a lake or the Tennessee River. In our sessions, Michael often wore a mask of arrogance and loved to distract me with wisecracks anytime we got close to exploring his inner terror and pain. As much as he liked to hide behind this cheeky facade, I was quite worried he would drop out of therapy if we didn't get a breakthrough soon. Worse, I was concerned he could be at high risk for suicide if he gave up on his goals or convinced himself that he couldn't be helped.

One day, Michael started the session by saying, "Ah, I see you're wearing new boots today. Is that what you do with the money from our sessions? Or are you wearing those because you think you're going to kick my butt today with some psycho-mumbo jumbo?"

If I directly confronted Michael with a statement such as "I wonder what prompted you to say that? Does it feel like relationships have to be a power struggle?" he would just scoff and skirt the issue. Instead, I learned the best way to motivate Michael was to welcome his humor into the session and be playful with him. Moreover, playing helped my own emotional brain calm down and avoid feeling threatened by his unnerving comments.

So I laughed when he teased me about my boots and replied, "Yeah.

I've got a challenge for you. I know you want to test me to see if I know what I'm doing and whether or not this therapy thing has been worth your money. I think you're ready to cross a few small bridges on foot between now and our next session. You can start out with the little footbridge that crosses the creek in the park a couple of blocks from my office. I'll even meet you there in my kick-ass boots, if you like."

He laughed and said in a mocking voice, "No, Miss Courtney, I don't need you to hold my hand. I can do it all by my wittle self."

I winked and goaded, "I know you can do it, but I bet you won't."

"I'll bet I will," he responded with a wry smile and added, "I'll take a picture on my phone to prove it to you, Miss Smarty Pants."

I shook my head. "I don't believe it. I bet you $50 you won't do it."

"You're on, lady," he said, shaking his fist at me. "If I do it, you'll give me $50 off this session?"

I nodded and said, "Yes, sir, I will. But I don't have to worry about it because you're so stubborn, I know you won't do it."

He leapt from the sofa. "Well, I'll go do it right now and show you! I want my $50!" With that he drove right over to the park, marched across the bridge, and texted me a picture of him standing on the other side with his tongue sticking out.

He returned to my office within 25 minutes, grinning from ear to ear. Since we still had a few minutes left in his session, I invited him to sit down and handed him $50. As he reached out to take the money, his hands were trembling and his face was flushed. He gave me a brief hug and began to cry. "Thank you," he said. "You got me all caught up in that. It's just now hitting me what I did. I really did it. I can do this."

I smiled, and said, "Yes, Michael, you absolutely can. We just had to find something more emotionally compelling than your fear to get you to take a risk."

Over time, a series of similar therapeutic experiences we did together revealed the deeper root of his fears—a long-held presumption that people and the world would always hurt and disappoint him. Once he could put words to this nonverbal, deeply felt reality that had been overshadowing everything in his life, it became less daunting to him. In our last session, he commented, "Yeah, people can hurt and disappoint you. Nothing is ever guaranteed in life, but you do the best you can. The *experience* of going for what I want is still worth it. I can at least believe in that."

Mind you, if I made bets like this with all my clients, I'd be broke. The point I want to make is that sometimes we have to cajole clients into doing what is in their best interest. You do this not so much by coming up with a playful intervention, but by maintaining a playful *attitude*. I had no idea what I was going to do in Michael's session before he arrived that day. But when he began by poking fun at me, I decided to mirror his teasing—realizing the only way I could get around his resistance was to align with it. Otherwise, he'd make me part of his struggle.

When you can act out the client's resistance in a funny, nonthreatening way, it puts *him* in the position of arguing for change. Furthermore, the guise of joking around allows clients like Michael to "save face" while trying out new skills.

PRIMING WITH ROLE-PLAY

Associative role-play games are also good for diffusing apprehension and building the client's confidence as he or she tries out new behaviors. The emotional brain learns from association and takes over what we consciously repeat. We know it's a good idea to rehearse new behaviors with clients in the session, but when you add a bit of fun and novelty to it, your clients will be even more likely to remember new responses and try them at home.

My training in RRT inspired the association games that follow, and it still amazes me (and my clients) how quick and effective these humorous games are at diffusing anxiety and relieving feelings of guilt and resentment. To introduce a role-play game, I usually say to clients, "I learned a trick that seems silly, but it will get your mind to produce the response you want more automatically. Would you like for me to it show you?" Usually, the client eagerly says, "Yes! What is it?" Clients are much more receptive to the idea of being playful and silly if you give them a choice.

To set up a role-play game, ask yourself, "What response has my client's mind been producing, and how do I want his mind to respond instead?" In cognitive therapy this is called identifying negative thoughts and replacing them with neutral or positive thoughts. But, as you now know, identifying and replacing thoughts at the rational level won't fix the problem. You also have to reach the emotional brain, which learns through association and a novel, emotionally infused experience.

Remember Teresa, the client from Chapters 2 and 4 who couldn't stop worrying about her son relapsing? When someone is obsessively worrying, it's because the emotional brain is scanning for threat and trying to get the person to *stop* the imagined event from happening. Once the emotional brain realizes the event is not happening and that there is nothing that needs to be done, it will turn off the emotional urge to take an action. In essence, Teresa's emotional brain had been saying, "Quick! Monitor everything your son Bobby is doing 24/7, so he doesn't use drugs. Do it now!" The response we wanted her mind to generate was, "I can't monitor everything Bobby is doing. I've provided him with plenty of resources. There is nothing else I need to do right now." We designed a role play based on these statements to reinforce associative learning of this new response at the level of the emotional brain.

To make the role play livelier, I invited Teresa to think of a funny character that could represent the aspect of her mind that was constantly scanning for threat. She smiled and immediately said, "Gladys Kravitz, the nosy neighbor off the 1970s comedy show, *Bewitched.* That lady constantly stared out the window, spying on people, looking for trouble. And that's exactly what my mind's been doing—looking for trouble."

Therapist: [laughing with client] Oh, yes! That image is perfect. Okay, I'll play Gladys Kravitz and I'm going to ask you to do things that you realize you don't need to do anything about. You reply by saying, "There's nothing I need to do about that right now." Some things will be obvious, some not so obvious, but the answer is the same. Got it?

Teresa: Yeah, I got it.

Therapist: There's a donkey in the neighbor's living room. Do something!
Teresa: [laughing] There's nothing I need to do about that right now.
Therapist: Miley Cyrus is twerking again. Make it stop!
Teresa: (shaking her head) Definitely nothing I can do about that!
Therapist: Well, get her father to stop her from gyrating her butt like that. It's disgusting.
Teresa: Nothing he nor I can do about that right now. Miley's an adult.

Once the client has the gist of the game down with these campy scenarios, then ask her to apply the same answer as you deliver a few statements regarding her real-life situation.

Therapist: Your son didn't call yesterday. Get him to call you right now.
Teresa: Nothing I need to do about that right now.
Therapist: Well, get him to have not used drugs in the past. Hurry!
Teresa: There's nothing I need to do about that. I can't go back to the past.
Therapist: Well, make sure he doesn't have a pill in his mouth right now.
Teresa: Nothing I can do about that. He lives 500 miles away.

We went through a few more rounds of this role play until Teresa felt the new response was coming to her automatically and authentically. Starting the role play by asking Teresa to stop a celebrity's dancing was intended to establish an absurd association with an event that she clearly could not stop. Moreover, pairing an unexpected, laughable image causes the client's feared scenario to seem less realistic and threatening. I used the scenario of Miley's dancing because it was an humorous example of another young person doing something risky that her parents probably don't like but realize they can't stop.

Role plays also work well when you want to help a client decrease codependent behavior, develop assertiveness, or feel more comfortable saying "no." Leslie was a client who had difficulty refusing a friend who kept asking her for money. Leslie knew logically that she needed to deny her friend's request and was feeling very frustrated with her repeated acquiescence to these requests. Here is the role play I created for Leslie:

Therapist: I know that saying "no" to your friend has not been comfortable, but I have a game we can play that will help you feel more confident in your ability to do this. I'm going to play your friend asking you for money and you say, "I'm not in a position to do that." No matter what I say, you just keep giving me that same answer.

Leslie: Okay.

Therapist: Leslie, they turned my power off and I need to borrow $100 from you.

Leslie: I'm so sorry, but I don't have it right now.

Therapist: Come on! I saw a $100 bill in your wallet.

Leslie: Well, that's to pay my bills. I can't give it to you because my phone bill is due and my parents will get mad if I ask them for more money. I'm really, really sorry.

As you can see, the first time we went through the role play, Leslie fell into her usual pattern of over-apologizing and doing a lot of unnecessary explaining to justify her reluctance to loan money to her friend. To help Leslie realize how these statements reflected uncertainty in her resolve, we switched roles, with me repeating the statements the way she said them to me. Afterward, Leslie commented, "Oh my gosh, you're right. When you apologized and gave me all these excuses for not loaning me money, it made me feel like you really could give me the money if you wanted to."

We switched roles again as I coached, "See how it feels to adjust your posture, unclasp your hands, relax your shoulders, set your feet square on the floor, and say, 'I'm not in a position to do that' without adding any apologies or explanations. If it doesn't feel right to you, that's okay. It just means that there's some other emotional conflict about saying 'no' that we can explore."

Leslie: Yeah, there may be an internal conflict. But I want to try the role play again.

Therapist: Okay. Leslie, they turned my power off. I need $100 to pay the bill.

Leslie: I'm not in a position to do that.

Therapist: Come on! I saw a $100 bill in your wallet.

Leslie: I can't give you that.

Therapist: Don't you care about me? I'll pay you back next week.

Leslie: I care about you, but I'm not in a position to do that, so quit hassling me about it!

Therapist: Ah . . . you threw in a little attitude at the end of that one. How did that feel?

Leslie: [smiling] That was kind of fun. It actually feels much better to respond that way.

We elaborated on this role play with exaggerated gestures and movement to decrease anxiety and further reinforce Leslie's new behavior. I'll discuss integrating mindful movement in more detail in Chapter 10.

HEALING TRAUMA WITH HUMOR

When timed right and delivered respectfully, humor can alleviate anxiety, empower clients, and change the emotional meaning of traumatic memories. I used to worry that humor might offend clients who had experienced trauma, but most trauma survivors have a great sense of humor and cite it as one of their primary coping skills. Inviting them to be playful in sessions and look at their past through the lens of absurdity is often a relief and gives them a sense of mastery over the issue.

One of the primary ways I use humor when treating trauma is to collaboratively retell the story with the client as we exaggerate all the bizarre elements of the event. It's not hard to make a trauma story bizarre because the very definition of trauma is that it is something unusual that happens out of the realm of "normal" experience. Retelling the story in a ludicrous way is one way to neutralize unhelpful meanings that got attached to the event. You may recall I used this technique with my client Carol in Chapter 5 when I retold her story back to her with intentional errors.

As I demonstrated in Chapter 5 with Carol's story, before I suggest reconstructing the narrative in a nonsensical way, I allow the client to retell the trauma story from her perspective first, so she feels heard and respected. As you are listening to this first version of her story, listen for where she is still attaching distorted meanings about herself, others, or her future. Then, think of how you can recast the story as being an off-the-wall event that didn't mean anything about her, except that she was clever and strong enough to survive the darn thing.

For example, my client Leslie (from the earlier role-play example) had been sexually abused by her stepfather when she was a child. Even though her stepfather was not in her or her mother's life anymore, she still felt haunted by this event. She also thought it was the root of her tendency to comply with others' unreasonable demands and her fear that they would hurt her if she didn't go along.

When Leslie told her story to me the first time she stated, "My stepfather seemed like a giant as he stood over me and made me give him oral sex. I complied because I thought he'd hurt me worse if I didn't. I still feel so dirty and disgusted with myself when I think about it."

After listening to her account of what happened, I commended Leslie for getting through this event and acknowledged that going along with her stepfather's sexual demands was the less risky option for her at that time. I likened it to the way hostage negotiators subdue and comply with the initial demands of a man who threatens to bomb a school. I pointed out to her, "Hostage negotiators don't start by threatening to send the S.W.A.T team in all guns-a-blazing. That tactic would surely set an unstable person off and get all the children killed. Instead, they try to understand what he's upset about to subdue him, then they may even offer him a sandwich or something while they work on a strategy to get him out of the building. That's essentially what I think you did with your stepfather. You complied with his request in an effort to subdue him until it became possible for you and your mom to strategically remove this man from your lives." Leslie sighed with relief and agreed this perspective made sense to her.

Next I offered, "I'm going to tell the story back to you, and I'll get some things wrong on purpose. Your job is to correct me like I'm a dumb detective. It may seem kind of silly, but I think it will have you feeling much more on top of this thing." Leslie seemed intrigued at my suggesting this game as she leaned forward, smiled, and said, "Okay."

Initially, I repeated the story back to Leslie with a few innocuous errors, such as incorrectly stating her age and the time of day when the events occurred. Having Leslie focus on correcting me not only gave her a sense of control, but it also had her concentrating on the factual details of the event rather than reliving it emotionally. This conscious intention of getting the facts straight also helps integrate the event into explicit memory. Because Leslie was reacting well to correcting minor errors as I retold her story, I slipped in comical errors as we were getting to the parts of the story that previously made her uncomfortable. For instance, I said, "Your stepfather walked into your room and he was wearing a purple dress." Imagining this preposterous picture caused Leslie to laugh out loud and made the image of her stepfather less intimidating. He now seemed less like a scary giant and more like a loony-tune.

The other meaning I wanted to adjust for Leslie was her mistaken belief that she was dirty and disgusting. So I offered, "Your stepfather did weird stuff and he wanted you to do weird stuff. You didn't like doing that stuff with him. But you realized he was whacked, so you did what you had to do to get a crazy man out of your bedroom. Later, you took a shower and washed all of that off, so none of it got on you. That event is finished, completed, and defeated." Then, we slapped hands as I gave her a celebratory "high five" to acknowledge her survival was a victory of which she could feel proud rather than ashamed. She said she liked the *experience* of co-telling the story this way and was also surprised at how empowered she felt by receiving a high five at the end of it. Co-telling the story in a way that casts the client as a heroine doing the best she can with an insane situation is another way to create a mismatch experience that facilitates memory reconsolidation in Step 5 of the RECON process.

ADOPTING ACCENTS TO DIMINISH FEAR AND ANGER

Anger and fear are emotional and physiological responses to a perceived threat. Thus, the only way to get rid of fear or anger is to eliminate the perception of danger. Humor is a wonderful way to bring a menacing threat down to size. One way to temper disturbing material with comedy is to have the client sing or narrate his story in a funny voice. Not only does clowning around give the client a sense of mastery over his story, but it also can put the behavior of other people in a silly and less threatening light.

When you use humor in this way, you're not minimizing the client's problem. Rather, you are minimizing the effect the words and behavior of someone else has had on him. However, I don't invite a client to play these character games until we've gone through his story factually a time or two. Then, if I think the client would be open to a little tomfoolery, I introduce the strategy by saying, "I can teach you a game that's kind of silly, but it could have you feeling in more control of this memory. Would you like to give it a go?" Clients are usually curious and open to playing along. Granted, when I tell clients the game involves talking in a funny voice, they can display a bit of apprehension. If a client is not open to such playful interventions, I move on to something else and don't force it. But, if the client indicates interest and curiosity about this technique, I initiate the role-play by getting into character and speaking in a silly voice myself first. This usually prompts clients to join me in the fun.

For example, Ross was a screenwriter who was referred to me by his doctor to treat a severe needle phobia. Ross had a health condition that required blood to be drawn once a month. But the nurses had been unsuccessful in drawing blood because Ross would go into a full-blown panic attack at the sight of a needle.

At first Ross couldn't recall any particular event that caused his needle phobia. But, when we employed Step 2 of the RECON process to locate the root of an emotional response, a childhood memory emerged of a nurse who held Ross down and yelled at him while she attempted to draw blood from his arm. Ross felt a panic attack coming on midway through telling me this story. He began to sweat and gasp for air as he cried, "I don't think I can do this."

I remained calm and changed the subject momentarily by asking Ross to tell me about a screenplay he was writing until I noticed his anxiety dissipate. Then I suggested we go through the story of the traumatic event again. This time I suggested we take turns telling different parts of the story and speak in foreign accents.

His jaw dropped as he raised his eyebrows and asked, "What?"

I explained to Ross that I only suggested it because humor lessens anxiety and can make recounting a frightening story easier, but I reassured him we did not have to do it this way if he didn't want to. He agreed that his sense of humor had helped him cope with anxiety in the past and was open to co-telling the story as if we were acting out a screenplay together. To give Ross even more of a sense of control, I let him be the director and decide how the scene would play out and give me my lines.

Ross proposed that I play him as a boy in the scene and suggested I use a French accent. In turn, he would play the nurse and decided to give her a German accent. I began by saying, "Excusez moi, large-boned lady, but what is zis business of moving a sharp, pointy object toward my arm?"

Ross replied in his best German accent, "You vill allow me to insert dis needle into your arm and you vill like it, tiny Frenchman! When we are done, I vill give you a delicious strudel, and you vill like dis, too."

We went on with this role play through the entire story until we were both laughing hysterically. Once we gained our composure, I asked Ross to go through the story again in his regular voice. He was amazed that he was able to tell the story this time without any sign of panic. He also realized his fear was not so much of needles, but of not being in control. This led us to explore how his willingness to have his blood drawn could actually put him in control of his health. The next week, he successfully gave blood at his doctor's office and reports having no problems with it ever since.

In sum, research indicates that activating the PLAY emotional system fosters positive connections between people, decreases resistance, promotes a sense of mastery, and sparks creative problem solving. In fact, Panksepp opined, "any therapist who can capture the therapeutic moment in mutually shared play episodes will have brought the client to the gateway of happy living" (2009, p. 16).

Therapists can stimulate the PLAY system by initiating amusing role-play games that assist clients in making new associations, rehearsing new behaviors, and building confidence. Similarly, therapists can collaborate with clients to retell troubling stories with a humorous slant that places the client as a heroic character in a comedy of errors. Of course, not all people will be receptive to humor and play, so the therapist should check with the client to see if he is open to comedic interventions before proceeding. Fortunately, most clients are open to a bit of jocular diversion in the session and often gain spontaneous insight by accessing positive emotional states. You can also use music to help the client access positive emotional states and neutralize negative meanings, as we'll discuss in the next chapter, Rousing With Rhythm, Music, and Poetry.

CHAPTER 9

Rousing With Rhythm, Music, and Poetry

Music is a powerful way to evoke emotion, alter mood, and influence behavior, so much so that retail stores select background music designed to elicit positive moods and purchasing behaviors within their customers. I witnessed the persuasive power of music firsthand while working at a shoe store in undergraduate school. When we played upbeat music in the store like Soca, a soulful style of calypso, customers danced in the aisles, and we joyfully sold shoes all day long. But after a while we grew tired of listening to steel drums and decided to play blues music. Even though customers also swayed to these soulful rhythms, they seemed less pumped up about buying pumps. Sales plummeted. Ironically, we heard business increased at a bar near the store. We joked that after a few minutes of listening to the wails of Walter "Wolfman" Washington, our patrons must be thinking, "Ah, hell. Nobody loves me and I don't have any money," then saunter off to the bar down the street.

Although this example depicts the way music can negatively affect mood, you can teach your clients to use music in a way that positively influences them. In this chapter I'll explain how music and rhythm impact the brain and share easy ways to use music and poetry to facilitate emotional expression, lift disquieting moods, calm anxiety, and tap into deeper levels of insight.

MUSIC AND THE BRAIN

Neuroscience research has shown that listening to music stimulates activity in the reward and pleasure centers of the brain, even if the music is sad. For example, a 2005 study by Menon and Levitin examined brain responses to classical music using functional magnetic resonance imaging (fMRI) and found significant activation in the nucleus accumbens and ventral tegmental area (VTA). The VTA is critical for associative learning because it projects dopamine to the nucleus accumbens, which is considered the brain's reward center. Similarly, studies have shown that music releases endogenous opioids in the brain, particularly when we listen to a piece that evokes "thrills or chills" (Huron & Marguilis, 2010). In fact, a study by Goldstein in 1980 showed that the pleasure a person feels from listening to a piece of music can be blocked when an opioid antagonist like Naloxone is in the person's system. In addition to music's impact on the reward centers in the brain, the amygdala, insula, and orbitofrontal cortex are also involved in evoking emotional and physiological responses to song.

Even though brain imaging has identified these neural correlates, these discoveries didn't really explain *how* music evokes emotional responses in the brain. Thus, Juslin and Vastfjall (2008) developed the BRECVEM model that delineates seven brain mechanisms through which music can elicit emotion: (1) brain stem reflexes, (2) rhythmic entrainment, (3) evaluative conditioning, (4) emotional contagion, (5) visual imagery, (6) episodic memory, and (7) musical expectancy.

The *brain stem reflex* refers to a response triggered by a sound in a musical piece that signals an event that needs an urgent response, such as the thundering bang of cannons heard in Tchaikovsky's *1812 Overture*. The sound of loud, booming noises can certainly excite the sympathetic nervous system, even if we know there are no actual cannons threatening us. The second brain mechanism, *rhythmic entrainment*, refers to the influence of a song's beat on internal bodily rhythms such as heartbeat and breathing rate. I'll discuss the entrainment phenomenon in more detail later in this chapter and show you how to utilize entrainment to modify mood and induce relaxation. *Evaluative conditioning* refers to a piece of music evoking a particular emotion because it has been paired with a positive or negative stimulus. This is exemplified in The Amygdaloids' song "Reminds Me of You," which croons about the way a tune that a guy pleasantly associated with his lover now vexes the heck out of him because the relationship is over.

Emotional contagion refers to feelings that are evoked by the emotional expressiveness we hear in the music or voice of the singer. It's believed to be related to mirror neurons and the empathy we feel when someone shares a deeply felt experience with us. For instance, the ballad "I Will Always Love You" written by Dolly Parton can elicit moist eyes in even the most brawny guy whether it is sung by Dolly Parton or Whitney Houston. If that song doesn't pull at your heartstrings, then compositions like Beethoven's *Moonlight Sonata*, "The Sound of Silence" by Simon and Garfunkel, Sara McLaughlin's "Angel," or Sade's haunting song "Like a Tattoo" may stir you.

Ironically, a 2013 study by Kawakami et al. found that listening to sad music actually produces positive emotions. Although the researchers proposed further investigation be done to explain this outcome, they suggested melancholy music may not lead us to utter depression because we are feeling vicarious, rather than direct emotion. Daniel Levitin (2006), a neuroscientist and music researcher at McGill University, has reported that when humans sing together, their brains release oxytocin, a powerful hormone that promotes emotional bonding. Perhaps we also bond with one another when we are listening to sad music, which may explain why listening to a sad song feels strangely comforting.

For many people music can bring to mind *visual imagery* that evokes an emotional response. The Bonny Method of Guided Imagery and Music is based on this premise. With the Bonny Method, clients listen to carefully selected sequences of classical music and observe any imagery that emerges as they listen to the compositions. Research on this model has shown it has been helpful in treating trauma, decreasing substance abuse, and integrating subconscious, affectively charged material (Bruscia & Grocke, 2002). Not all people experience visual imagery while listening to music, however, so there are boundaries to this application.

Music is often associated with *episodic memories* of previous events or time periods of one's life. Therefore, music from a particular time period can be used intentionally to bring up emotional memories or produce nostalgic feelings of happier times. Music has the power to do this even for people with Alzheimer's disease, who often seem flat, disoriented, or unresponsive. In his book *Musicophilia*, Oliver Sacks (2007) shares several examples of the way music lifts the spirit and stimulates various cognitive processes of elderly people in nursing homes. I observed this same response working in a gero-psychiatric unit earlier in my career. Gathering patients to sing old hymns or listen to popular tunes of the 1920s, 30s, or 40s decreased agitation, improved mood, and facilitated social interaction.

Finally, music has the power to give us "chills and thrills," particularly when a specific portion of the piece deviates from what we would expect from the song's harmonic pattern. This is called *musical expectancy*. As we're listening to a piece of music, our brains track the rhythm, melody, and tempo and predict what will happen next. When an intense unexpected harmonic change occurs, such as a dramatic increase in loudness, it arouses both the sympathetic nervous system and reward systems in the brain. Led Zeppelin's "Stairway to Heaven" is a modern example of the way changes in music expectancy create thrills and chills. The composition starts out soft with an acoustic guitar and flute melody, and then escalates into an electrifying rock orchestra stimulating interest, excitement, and emotional anticipation. Levitin opined that the secret to creating engaging songs such as "Stairway to Heaven" is "to balance predictability and surprise" (2010, p. 834).

FACILITATING EMOTIONAL EXPRESSION THROUGH MUSIC

Given all the elements described earlier, music can be a powerful catalyst for clients who feel emotionally blocked or stuck. As a therapist who specializes in treating trauma and grief, I've learned music can be a more palatable way for clients to digest feelings they'd rather avoid. For example, hard-driving rock music can empower trauma survivors and provide a safe outlet for expressing anger. When clients use music to express anger, it's good to advise them to release their feelings through physical movement like dancing, running, or working out as they listen. Obviously, you don't want clients to use music to get all pumped up and unleash it in an unhealthy way on someone else or themselves.

In addition, it's useful to coach clients to arrange songs on a playlist so that the tempo gradually moves toward a calmer, more equable state, where they can find a sense of emotional resolution. For example, the song "Rearview Mirror" by Pearl Jam reflects the anger of someone who is escaping an abusive home, but it ends by affirming the satisfaction of leaving this phase of life behind and moving on.

Clients who enjoy playing an instrument often use their musical skills to express their feelings, so it's beneficial to incorporate their musical interest and talents into therapy. In his book *The Tao of Music*, psychologist John Oritz (1997) talked about a rebellious adolescent who was referred to him for anger management in a last attempt to avoid placement in a detention center. Although this young male client challenged Oritz during the first two sessions, he softened when he noticed Oritz had a guitar in his office. The boy told Oritz he'd always wanted to play the guitar, and they discussed how he might convince his parents to buy him one and let him take lessons. Within months of learning how to play the six-string, Oritz's client began playing a few chords and songs to vent his frustration. More important, he began writing his own songs, which helped him come to terms with deeper feelings of vulnerability that underlay his angry outbursts. Eventually the boy's feelings of fury diminished and he developed more amicable relationships with his peers.

Grieving clients who have been feeling numb or unable to cry can listen to a piece of music that reminds them of the deceased to help them release tears and foster a continuing bond. In her book *Music for the Soul*, musician and hospice educator Joy Berger (2006) discusses how therapists can assist clients in creating musical playlists for this purpose. Berger's suggestions for playlists include selecting the deceased's favorite pieces of music, music that gives voice to the griever's feelings of loss, and songs that engender hope for the future.

Likewise, in a therapy session, music can be used to reflect on how the deceased influenced the client; reconstruct the meaning of the loss; resolve unfinished business; and continue the bond with the deceased in a healthy way. Not only have my clients found creating these playlists healing, but I also found it helpful in dealing with my own grief. To my dismay, my father-in-law, Lynn, and my dog Buzz died while I was writing this book. My father-in-law was a gregarious man who had been our family's "rock" for many years and was full of love and humor. Similarly, Buzz was a vibrant yellow Labrador retriever who had a boundless enthusiasm for life and brought our family much joy. After Lynn and Buzz died, I not only grieved them but also found myself revisiting painful remnants of previous losses their presence had helped me assuage.

To ease my sorrow, I created what I call a "Mood Modifying Playlist" that began with songs that reflected my sadness, then progressed to songs about letting go, and concluded with songs about how I wanted to remember Buzz and Lynn and the things they taught me. The songs I chose are listed next. I share this list to give you an example of what a Mood Modifying Playlist might look like. Most of these songs are available via iTunes or as videos on YouTube if you would like to listen to any of them.

1. "Goodbye" by Patty Griffin—a folksy ballad about coming to terms with the pain of someone's death and longing for a "better way to say goodbye." Written and sung by Griffin, who has a gorgeous, emotionally expressive voice.
2. "I Grieve" by Peter Gabriel—a song that begins low and slow, then cries out in gut-wrenching pain as it echoes the shock and overwhelm one feels after loss, but ends with a soft, rhythmic upbeat and lyrics about carrying on with life.
3. "When the Snow Melts" by Phil Cunningham and Mànus Lunny—a peaceful instrumental with soothing guitar strums and reassuring flute melodies.

4. "In the Garden," performed by Susan Tedeschi and Double Trouble, written by C. Austin Miles—an old Christian hymn about the anticipated joy of entering Heaven and leaving suffering behind. Tedeschi and Double Trouble's remake of the song is very soulful, bluesy, and moving.
5. "Heavenly Day" by Patty Griffin—a sweet, joyful tune that Griffin says was inspired by the pleasure of hanging out with her dog and looking at life through her pup's carefree eyes.
6. "World Keeps Spinning" by Brand New Heavies—a very danceable R&B tune about acknowledging regrets, having faith that life will get better, and being open to feeling love again.

Listening to this playlist provided a roadmap for navigating my grief and was at once cathartic and uplifting. Although I sobbed deeply listening to the first two songs, the last two songs actually made me smile and feel like dancing.

Similarly, one of my clients found listening to intentionally selected music helped him deal with feelings of dread and despair after his son died. He was mildly responsive to the use of imagery and hypnosis in our sessions. But I realized music was the more powerful gateway to his emotions when he said the song "I Dreamed a Dream" from the musical *Les Misérables* perfectly reflected the dejection he felt. When I offered to play the song in a session, he protested, "No, no. Don't play it! Even though I love the song, listening to it completely levels me. If I hear it, I'll be a wreck for the rest of the day."

This led us to a general discussion about how music affects mood and an exploration of songs that might engender a better frame of mind for him. His feelings of hopelessness were the worst when he awoke in the morning, so he decided to make a playlist he could listen to while taking his morning walks. He began by pulling a few songs from his son's favorite artists, then added his own preferred music. After months of feeling immobilized by his grief, listening to this playlist each day became a valuable tool that helped him move forward.

MODIFYING MOOD WITH PLAYLISTS

When crafting a therapeutic music playlist, it can be helpful to start with 1 or 2 songs in a tempo that match the client's current emotional state. Then, select 3 or 4 songs that gradually progress toward a tempo that reflects the client's *desired* emotional state. This suggestion is based on the concept of entrainment. Entrainment occurs when one object's oscillatory movement synchronizes with the rhythm of another object's rhythmic movement. Christiaan Huygens, the Dutch scientist who invented the pendulum clock, documented this phenomenon around 1665 when he observed that two pendulum clocks sitting side by side would fall into a synchronous rhythm with one another. Physicists speculate that two or more objects within close range enter into this harmonic movement because it is a more stable and efficient use of energy. In other words, it takes less effort to "go with the flow" of a dominant tempo than to continue bumping up against it.

We see this in the therapeutic relationship when we align, lift, and lead with a client. As discussed in Chapter 2, you first tune into the cadence of the client's current state and empathically synchronize your communication with his or her rhythms. But, if you let the client's distressed state set the tone of the entire session, you can both end up feeling depressed. Thus, it behooves you to initially pace with the swing of the client's emotional pendulum, then gradually lead the client into a more positive rhythmic state. The same concept applies with music.

Oritz (1997) suggests the ideal playlist for entrainment contains about 30 minutes of music, which amounts to about six or seven songs. As stated earlier, the playlist should begin with a song or two that echoes the timbre of the client's current mood, and then gradually progress to songs that elicit the client's desired affective state. Clients may say they prefer to jump right into inspiring music to lift their moods, and sometimes this works. But when someone is really feeling blue or angry, uplifting music can be downright irritating. If you don't believe me, try listening to "Don't Worry Be Happy" by Bobby McFerrin the next time you're feeling really agitated. Then tell me if it doesn't drive you up a wall!

Because people vary in their musical tastes, the research shows it's best if the client chooses his own songs for the playlist. Many clients already have a collection of favorite tunes on their Smartphones and can scroll through potential selections during the session. Alternatively, if you have a computer and Internet access in your office, then it's easy to look up a few of the client's chosen songs and play samples of them in the session. Although you can start crafting the playlist in the session, the client will likely need to continue building his playlist at home. Invite your client to bring his playlist to the next session to play it for you. This shared experience of listening to music that is personally meaningful during a session is very therapeutic.

ENTRAINING TO ALPHA-THETA STATES

You can also use music to entrain the brain to calmer states and deeper levels of consciousness. Research shows that certain rhythmic arrangements and tones lead the brain to produce alpha and theta brain wave patterns, the states associated with relaxation, intuition, creativity, and healing. The alpha-theta brain wave states are also reached through meditation practice and have been shown to improve emotional regulation by strengthening connections between the emotional brain and medial prefrontal cortex (Brefczynski-Lewis et al., 2007; Hölzel et al., 2011). Furthermore, research suggests that we more readily receive and integrate new information when our brain waves are oscillating at an alpha or theta wave frequency (Kershaw & Wade, 2012.) Therefore, facilitating these deeper states of awareness often leads to profound insights and creative problem solving.

Music with a tempo of around 60–70 beats per minute is associated with alpha-theta states because it corresponds to the rhythm of a relaxed human heartbeat. Playing this slower speed of music in the background while facilitating guided imagery, hypnosis, or mindfulness techniques is especially helpful for anxious clients. Focusing on the music seems to distract them from ruminating thoughts, promotes a sense of safety, and fosters positive affective states as it deepens trance. However, music therapist Janalea Hoffman (1995) suggests extremely keyed-up clients can more effectively relax if the musical tempo begins by matching the rhythm of their alert, tense state and gradually moves to a slower pace. She developed instrumental music for this purpose that moves from 80 beats per minute to 50 beats per minute.

In addition to Janalea Hoffman's music, I also recommend music by Steve Halpern and the founder of the Center for Neuroacoustic Research, Jeffrey Thompson. Not only are these artists talented musicians, but they have also grounded their compositions in sound research (*pun intended*). That said, there are hundreds of other musicians and composers who create music designed to induce relaxation and support deeper levels of consciousness. As stated earlier, studies have consistently shown that people relax best to music that they select themselves. So it's a good idea to invite the client to bring in her own music or at least allow her to choose what she likes from the selections you have available in your office.

RHYTHMIC RHYMES AND POETRY

As clients look for songs that evoke their desired emotional response, they may find a set of lyrics they can sing or hum that tend to work more effectively than standard self-talk interventions. For instance, one of my clients reduced anxiety and lessened feelings of depression by singing the song "Day by Day" from the musical *Godspell* in the mornings while taking a shower. This is sort of a musical spin on employing affirmations to combat negative thinking. Adding rhyme, song, and rhythm cranks affirmations up a notch because these employ both verbal and emotional areas of the brain. I call them "affirmations with an attitude."

Clients can also calm anxiety by creating humorous rhymes and songs to recite when panic strikes. For example, a client with social anxiety came up with an affirmation she sang to the tune of "We're Not

Gonna Take It" by Twisted Sister. Whenever she felt the pangs of panic sensations in her chest, she'd sing, *"I'm not gonna panic/No! I'm not gonna panic/I'm not gonna panic anymore!"* Imagining the lipstick-wearing, big-haired band members of Twisted Sister simultaneously empowered her and made her laugh. She reasoned that if those guys felt comfortable going out in public dressed like that, she could feel okay going out in public, too.

Finally, poetry can be a powerful way for clients to express their feelings and find emotional resolution. One client who wrote rather dark poetry told me that although his verses sounded bleak, he actually felt more hopeful and relieved after getting his feelings out on paper. Writing the poetry also helped him stop self-mutilating because it became a healthier way for him to give voice to and externalize his internal pain.

My client Jana, the mother of a disabled child, illustrates another poignant example of the way poetry can transform emotional pain. Jana loved her daughter but felt very challenged by her daughter's limitations. Jana was very responsive to the use of imagery and metaphor in our sessions and felt compelled to expand on her experiences by writing poems. Through her poetry, Jana began to view the struggle to accept her daughter as mirroring her lifelong struggle to accept herself. Her poetry flourished as she turned her frustrations into metaphorical lessons and spiritual insights. Following is one of her poems entitled "Birth" that she has given me permission to share in this book:

Birth

The body, ravaged with turbulence, volume blaring of old records, the taunt of past mishaps flash across the mind's screen. A quake shivers my soul; like prey, the body weakens beneath being sought.

Passion, like a wild ocean wave, pushed its way towards a secure door. Tremors made headway; something endured and allowed—an opening. There it is, I have fallen into my heart.

I hear its blood-curdling scream like a new born whose breath trembles.

While helpless, yet helped, what once steadied me, severed.
Old rock-like framework became grit; time-crusted ideas
became liquid that splashed, poured sideways to wet my face
. . . the panting softened, I found the ground beneath my back;
movement was leery. . . still safe.

Jana said this poem expressed the terror she felt letting go of old beliefs that, although restrictive, provided structure to her life. The writing helped her pass through this tunnel of fear toward an opening of pure love and acceptance, which was at once refreshing and overwhelming. Jana also started daily mindfulness meditation and yoga practice while we were working together and commented, "When I create a breathing space, that's when the intelligence comes through. That's what I have learned to do with my daughter, too, give her the breathing space to pause and reflect on her behavior rather than thinking I have to constantly correct her." Jana also started expressing herself in a blog she created called *Raising Annie*. The title was inspired by Helen Keller's teacher Annie Sullivan, based on the irony that the people we think that we are teaching are, in fact, teaching us. I have to agree; Jana has taught me how to better listen for the inner wisdom that emerges in the "breathing space" between our thoughts and emotions. To read Jana's writing, you can visit her blog at http://janamassey95.wordpress.com.

Poetry and Songwriting Prompts

Of course, not everyone is going to have the natural talent for writing poetry that Jana has, but there are poetry prompts you can use for clients who seem open to this medium. One of my favorite ways to prompt poetic metaphors comes from the "Virtual Dream" exercise developed by grief therapy experts Douglas Smith and Robert Neimeyer. In his book *Techniques of Grief Therapy*, Neimeyer (2012) suggests providing a list of metaphorical elements and invites the client to select six of the elements and create a story, poem, or "virtual dream" from them. For example, one of my clients found this process helpful for working through her grief after her friend committed suicide. She crafted the following poem after selecting these six metaphorical elements from a collection of photo cards that I have in my office: (1) empty house, (2) cold wind, (3) dark shadow, (4) eagle, (5) rainbow, and (6) light ray.

> She sat in the empty house waiting for him to come.
> A cold wind blew and the dark shadow appeared.
> Though terrified, she approached, engulfed in the shadow's curious darkness.
> As she got to the edge, she realized the eagle cast the shadow.
> He invited her to ride and they rose to the sky,
> Embraced by a bright, calming light.
> From the sky she could see the world from a whole new perspective.
> Her light not broken, but now refracted into a rainbow.
> Signaling gratitude to all those who loved her, even in her darkness.

Neimeyer (2012) suggests that of the six elements, two should refer to the setting of the narrative, two should be symbolic of characters in the client's story, and the other two could represent symbolic objects or events. I have let clients pull interesting photos from magazines for this purpose. You can also purchase a deck of *Chi Ji* cards, which are a set of cards with metaphoric illustrations on them that are sold at many outlets that carry therapeutic games and supplies. Using these metaphorical prompts almost always turns out useful insights and poetic writing, even if the client does not think she is creative or has no prior experience with poetic expression.

If your client is more comfortable reading existing poetry rather than writing her own, that is fine, too. The therapeutic value of poetry has been recognized since Aristotle's time and was even acknowledged by Freud as a special form of writing that taps into unconscious material and gives voice to unexpressed feelings. Jung, Adler, Fritz Perls, J. L. Moreno, and other expressive therapy practitioners advocated the use of reading or writing poetry for catharsis and healing.

Why are we drawn to poetry? Pennebaker and Evans observed, "Unlike straight prose writing, poetry often captures the contradictions of emotions and experiences" (2014, Chapter 10, para. 14). Moreover, poems often contain metaphors that more aptly reflect complex emotional material. According to cognitive scientist George Lakoff, our cognition is not as linear as we think; he believes that we organize our understanding of the world through metaphor (Lakoff & Johnson, 2003). Poetry, it seems, is a natural language for the soul.

In his book *Poetry Therapy: Theory and Practice*, Mazza (2003) provides a number of examples of poems that are useful for processing in therapy sessions such as Robert Frost's "The Road Not Taken" or Marge Piercy's "Rape." Yet, just as with music, people have varying tastes for poetry. Younger people are likely to be drawn to "slam poetry" and hip-hop verses, whereas others may love classics by Emily Dickinson or Shakespeare. Therefore, it's best to let the client bring poems he or she finds meaningful to the session. In addition, consider your intention when processing poetry with your client. While Piercy's poem "Rape" may powerfully express the disgust and anger a person feels after sexual assault, it could also exacerbate one's sense of rage and hopelessness if merely taken as it is. Thus, it's important to explore what the poem means to the client. Following is a list of questions you can use to process a poem or a song with your clients.

- What does the poem or song mean to you?
- Does the poem/song provide a sense of validation or relief?
- How does it impact you to see the words on a page or hear the words out loud?
- Is there a specific line or aspect of the poem/song that spoke to you most?
- Does it leave you feeling better or worse about your experience?

- Would you add anything to the poem/song or change anything about it?
- How would you like the person in the poem/song to feel or think about himself or his situation now?
- Can you show the same compassion for yourself that you have for the writer?
- What kind of follow-up poem or letter would you write back to the writer?

In sum, music, rhythm, and poetry arouse our emotional centers and have the power to comfort, soothe, and change our moods. Brain research now validates that most music, even sad music, activates pleasure centers of the brain and has the ability to modulate our neurotransmitters and brainwave patterns. You can use music to facilitate emotional expression for clients who feel affectively blocked or stuck. Clients can also create musical playlists that can help them work through emotional pain. When creating a playlist, its useful for clients to begin with songs that match their moods and slowly transition to songs that evoke the feelings they desire. Likewise, clients can listen to music with a tempo of 50–60 beats per minute to entrain brain waves to slower alpha-theta states that induce relaxation and meditative states.

Because rhythm and rhyme enhance the ability to remember information and evoke positive emotional states, clients can use phrases and tunes from songs to anchor desired beliefs and affirmations. Last, poetry can be a way to translate implicit feeling states into explicit expression and awareness. You can provide metaphorical prompts that inspire clients to create their own poems or invite clients to explore poetry from other sources as a means of processing complex feelings.

Sometimes complex, implicit feelings defy words altogether and are better expressed through nonverbal means. In the next chapter, I'll present a variety of ways you can facilitate emotional resolution by integrating mindful movement.

CHAPTER 10

Integrating Mindful Movement

Incorporating body awareness and physical movement is another way to change implicit patterns and create breakthroughs for your clients. Perls and Miller (2013) recognized this many years ago and emphasized body awareness and movement as an integral part of Gestalt therapy. Somatically focused interventions are especially relevant for clients who have trouble tuning into deeper feelings; hold their bodies in tense or powerless postures; struggle with recurring overactive responses; or have physiological complaints related to past trauma. In fact, trauma expert Peter Levine (1997) believes an explicit narrative of a traumatic event cannot even be formed until the implicit aspects of it are accessed and processed somatically.

Recall that implicit memory involves the perceptual cues, somatic sensations, and procedural learning acquired during an emotional event. The brain learned the pattern through an *embodied experience*, so it often takes an embodied experience to unlearn or update the pattern. Grigsby and Stevens (2000) echoed this when they asserted that changing ingrained behaviors requires observing, interrupting, and replacing what has been procedurally learned rather than talking about how the patterns were formed.

Therapists intuitively know this, yet many clinicians are unsure of how to integrate physical movement, especially within the confines of a small office space. Therapists also feel unsure as to what kind of movement is "safe" or worry that engaging the client in movement could inadvertently exacerbate physical pain. One way to avoid this is to always ask the client if it would be okay to integrate body awareness and movement into the session before you start. If the client is receptive, ask him to immediately let you know if any movement feels uncomfortable or if he prefers not to engage in a certain movement. The physical actions I suggest in this chapter involve small mindful movements that are designed to give the client a sense of control. In addition, these are movements that most anyone can do, even in a modest office space.

CHANGING POSTURE CHANGES PERCEPTION

Just as our emotional states change the postures of our bodies, altering our postures can change emotional states. The most cited study about this phenomenon comes from the "Pencil Smile Study" performed by Strack, Martin, and Stepper in 1988. In this study, researchers showed cartoons to a group of participants who held a pencil between their teeth with their lips lifted into a smile position, while another group looked at the same cartoons holding the pencil tightly between pursed lips. As predicted, the subjects who held the pencil between their teeth with the smile position found the cartoons more amusing and reported a slight improvement in mood, whereas the other group did not find the cartoons as funny and reported a slight decrease in mood.

More recently, studies have investigated how body language affects our neurochemistry. For instance, Carney, Cuddy, and Yap (2010) demonstrated that participants who were instructed to hold an expansive, open posture that reflected power for just 2 minutes increased their levels of testosterone 20%, decreased cortisol levels by 25%, and were more open to taking risks. In contrast, participants who were instructed to hold a closed, contracted posture for 2 minutes demonstrated a 10% decrease in testosterone, a 15% increase in cortisol, and were more reluctant to take risks.

Another study published by Cuddy, Wilmuth, and Carney in 2012 demonstrated that people performed better in a mock interview when they held two power poses for 1 minute each prior to the interview. The first pose involved participants standing with feet shoulder width apart and placing their hands on their hips. The second pose involved participants sitting with their feet propped up on a desk, with their hands behind their head. In contrast, participants who held contracted postures for 2 minutes performed worse in the mock interviews. In the low-power postures, participants sat or stood with their feet crossed at the ankles and their hands crossed over their hips or knees.

What are the implications for therapy? First, these studies suggest the value of assisting clients in being more mindful of the way their body language could be affecting their interpersonal communication, self-esteem, and mood. Secondly, it suggests that coaching clients to alter their facial expressions, postures, and body language in the session can change their perceptions of themselves, a traumatic memory, and how they feel in general. As researcher Amy Cuddy stated in her 2012 TED talk, the findings of this and similar posture studies give credence to the maxim, "Fake it 'til you make it."

To coach a client toward a more powerful pose, encourage her to sit or stand with a broad, upright, open posture. This might include holding the head high, easing the shoulders back, and opening the chest. Cuddy and her colleagues found that open, relaxed, expansive postures were associated with confidence and power, whereas postures that are closed or contracted as if the person is "wrapping herself up" are associated with feeling threatened or powerless. Moreover, these nonverbal cues have been consistent across time and cultures, as Mehrabian (2007) demonstrated with his research, William James discussed in 1932, and Darwin (1899) ascertained through his studies on social behavior in both humans and animals in the 19th century.

My client Leslie from Chapter 8 is a good example of a person whose body language was undermining her self-esteem and her efforts to assert herself. When we did the role play that practiced saying "no" to her friend's request for money, Leslie began by sitting with her shoulders drawn in and her arms crossed over her waist. She slightly bowed her head as she recited in a soft, uncertain tone, "I'm not in a position to do that right now." We tried it again and I suggested she sit with her feet square on the floor, roll her shoulders back, lift her head up, and look directly at me. With this grounded, open posture, Leslie's voice immediately became stronger and clearer. She was amazed at the way this slight change in posture improved her ability to express herself. As we continued practicing, I got playful with her and suggested we exaggerate our postures and voices to sound like Valley Girls to further reduce her anxiety. Leslie really enjoyed this and said adding the humor made it more memorable and less threatening. Consequently, she was more comfortable saying "no" to her friend without making a big deal out of it.

As discussed in Chapter 8 on using play and humor in therapy, you can suggest clients take on more powerful poses or personas while retelling the story of the traumatic event. Even if the client pretends to be a completely absurd fictitious character like Darth Vader or Roseanne Rosannadanna, the corresponding attitude and physical gestures empower the client and reduce anxiety. Infusing this kind of humor is not intended to minimize the client's feelings but to give the client a sense of mastery and emotional distance from the event. Acting out such roles can also create a mismatch experience that reconsolidates a traumatic memory with a new meaning.

REPROCESSING TRAUMA THROUGH MOVEMENT

Guiding your client to engage in mindful movements that complete a survival response also promotes mastery, resilience, and reconsolidation after trauma. Body-based psychotherapies such as Peter Levine's (1997) somatic experiencing, Pat Ogden's (Ogden & Minton, 2006) sensorimotor therapy, and Ron Kurtz's (1990) Hakomi therapy all emphasize altering affective responses via "bottom-up" interventions that connect through the body.

As discussed in Chapter 1, all primary emotions prompt action tendencies in the body that want to be expressed. Levine and Ogden believe people with posttraumatic stress never got to complete or discharge the energy that was mobilized for survival and are stuck in the midst of a "freeze" response. The completion of the survival response seems to signal to the body that the person is out of danger and that the event is finished. In the wild, after a threat from a predator has passed, animals complete the survival response by shaking for several minutes as they mimic movements like running or fighting. Then, the animal appears to return to its baseline state and go on with its business. Likewise, supporting clients as they complete the survival actions their bodies wanted to take can heal traumatic stress so they can go on with their lives.

In Ogden and Minton's book, *Trauma and the Body: A Sensorimotor Approach to Psychotherapy* (2006), the authors explain that the therapist's role is to track the client's nonverbal cues and facilitate the client's awareness of his own sensations and movements. To aid the client in this process, Ogden suggests asking questions such as "What sensation do you feel in your body as you remember this incident? What happens inside your hand as it makes a fist?" Such prompts bring the client's attention to how the experience has been organized at the level of implicit, procedural memory. In addition, it redirects the client to maintain awareness of the present moment so he does not relive the traumatic event. The therapist may encourage the client to carry out "the movement that wants to happen" in the body so it can complete the survival response. However, Ogden advises that the therapist move slowly and assist the client in remaining within his "window of tolerance" for sympathetic arousal. The window of tolerance refers to the range of autonomic arousal the client can comfortably tolerate while reviewing emotionally charged material.

As discussed in Chapters 4 and 5, too much arousal of the sympathetic nervous system can retraumatize the client, while too little arousal may not bring enough implicit material to the surface for reprocessing. Therefore, you want to collaborate with the client to find the optimal balance between activating enough sensation to be in touch with the implicit aspects of the memory while maintaining awareness of his current surroundings so he doesn't relive the event. Coaching the client to move slowly and maintain dual awareness of the memory and the current moment achieves this.

For example, a client who left a physically abusive relationship complained of anxiety, insomnia, and chronic neck pain. Her gait was stiff and she had a tendency to hold her shoulders up toward her ears. She was receptive to using imagery, meditation, and relaxation techniques in our sessions, but she never felt like she could fully relax her muscles. When reprocessing one of her traumatic memories during Step 4 of the RECON process, I noticed she had a tendency to pull her shoulders up and freeze in the middle of the story with her head slightly turned to the right. This was the point in her story where her boyfriend backed her into a corner and began beating her face with his fist. I asked her to scan her body when she got to this part of the narrative and tell me what it felt like her body wanted to do. She noticed her head wanted to turn all the way to the right as her arms came up to shield her face. She realized that she had attempted to make this gesture before her boyfriend started hitting her, but she didn't get her hands up before he threw the first punch. I asked her to repeat the motion a few times while imagining that she had successfully blocked his punch. After doing this for a few minutes, she noticed her neck and shoulders began to loosen and relax.

Although this shielding move felt protective to her, we also explored moves that would help her feel empowered. As I guided her to continue following her body's impulses, she leaned forward, extended her arms, and said, "I want to push him back!" We stood and faced each other as I coached her to play this gesture out. I slowly moved my arm toward her face as she caught my arm and pushed it out of the way. Then, I encouraged her to extend her arms out in front of her body and walk toward me like she was pushing me while I backed away. We repeated these moves several times in the session as a means of facilitating positive mismatch experiences. Afterward, I asked her to retell her story and finish her narrative with the day she walked away from this relationship, then lift her arms up in a V-formation, signaling the "victory pose." Putting her arms up in the V-formation caused her to smile and reconnect to a sense of mastery. By the end of the session, her neck pain diminished significantly, and she was able to sleep more soundly in the weeks that followed.

Acting out triumphant gestures physically, like this client did with the victory pose, helps to change the meaning assigned to the story and the client's self-image. Pierre Janet believed that one of the reasons trauma haunts people is because they were not able to perform actions that signaled triumph over an adversity. Assisting clients to initiate movements that promote a sense of victory, competence, or mastery can transform their narratives of helplessness into a courageous account of resilience. Even if your client does not feel like she did anything triumphant, help her see that surviving the event was a victory in itself. Bring her awareness to when she was able to complete even the smallest act of self-care and escape from danger, such as leaving the scene of the event, dressing herself, completing school, or going back to work.

One client who was repeatedly sexually abused by her father could not identify any way that she had been triumphant until I brought her awareness to the day she asked for her bedroom to be moved when she was 11 years old. Moving her bedroom closer to her parents' room stopped her father's midnight visits because her mother could now hear what was going on. After I pointed out that this was a clever, courageous act on her part, she began to identify other ways she had quietly set boundaries and stood up for herself. Every time she identified another way she had set boundaries, I'd give her a high-five or a fist-bump to reinforce her feelings of competence and mastery. She enjoyed this game in the session and said it caused her to notice events in her life that she handled quite competently. Before this experience, she was only attending to moments when she felt like a failure.

Intentional hand gestures like the "high-five" or the "fist-bump" affirm clients and strengthen the therapeutic alliance. In fact, hand gestures can be useful in evoking a variety of desired emotional responses. For example, placing a hand over one's heart is a gesture that signals comfort and compassion, while placing one's hand on the solar plexus signals protecting one's boundaries. I've had clients practice both these gestures with mindful breathing as a way to bring themselves to the present moment and foster an internal sense of empowerment and self-compassion.

RESOLVING TRAUMA THROUGH DANCE

Another client named Maddie processed her trauma through improvisational dance. When Maddie was a teenager, she had been the victim of a gang rape by four boys from her school and was still carrying a great deal of shame, guilt, and rage around the incident well into her 30s. The idea of processing her feelings through dance came to her when she was selecting a playlist of songs we could use to help her work through her traumatic experiences. As Maddie was listening to the various songs at home, the dance moves spontaneously came to her and she proceeded to choreograph them into a short dance performance. She had been a professional dancer and discovered that using dance to reprocess this event reached a place in her soul that words could never venture.

Her playlist began by depicting the naive innocence, excitement, and optimism of a child with the illustrious show tune, "Everything's Coming up Roses." Then, the scene transitioned to Billy Idol's "Rebel Yell," reflecting the lightness, fun, and excitement of being a cheerleader in high school. Yet Maddie explained the song also symbolized the way she and her friends were discovering how to use their sexual power, mostly through flirting and dancing a little sexier as they cheered. Maddie clarified, "I never wanted to use that power other than to find somebody to love me. But women learn to play the game and use this power to get what they think they want." The music and dance then spiraled downward into the horrific gang rape she experienced at a daytime swimming pool party. She chose the song "Fat Bottomed Girls" by Queen for this scene, reflecting the randy, entitled attitude the boys used to justify their sexual aggressiveness toward her. Next, the dance meandered through her tormented journey for years after the incident, vacillating between rage and shame as she continued to look to others for love and acceptance.

I noticed that Maddie had several songs about feeling exploited and ended her dance script with a song about redemption and "Unwell" by Matchbox Twenty. Puzzled by these choices, I asked, "I'm curious about these last songs about redemption and being unwell? In my mind, you didn't do anything wrong. What do you think you need to be redeemed from?" Maddie widened her eyes and dropped her jaw as she exclaimed, "Wow, you're right. I'm still carrying guilt as if dancing like a cheerleader caused this incident. I'm going to revise this."

When Maddie returned to the next session, she commented, "Most of the songs in the original dance piece no longer resonate strongly for me anymore. They are like pieces of a puzzle that I have worked. They still fit in the big picture, but I am done with them." Even though this particular trauma felt resolved, Maddie realized that she had a desire to fight against the oppression of women and update the immature way our society portrays sex and sexual expression. She felt like she could do this through her professional artwork and choreographing a new dance performance about this issue. In addition, Maddie volunteered to pose nude for a life drawing class and found this experience empowering. To stand naked before a room full of people who did not attack or exploit her, but instead sought to represent her body in a respectful, beautiful light restored Maddie's dignity.

Getting Up to Calm Down

Maddie couldn't fully relax and process her feelings until she discharged her emotional energy through movement. This can be especially true for those who've experienced trauma because relaxing feels like they are leaving their bodies vulnerable to danger. In fact, trauma expert Babette Rothschild (2010) reports that 4% of the general population becomes more anxious when they attempt to relax. Of course, Maddie was comfortable moving through dance because she had experience as a professional dancer. I've also invited clients to do light stretching, Qi Gong, or walking around the office to relieve anxiety and lift their energy. In fact, if someone is really keyed up or agitated, inviting him to move with you a few minutes will bring the hyperarousal down more quickly than having him sit on your couch attempting to relax. Sometimes the body needs to work out the excess adrenalin of a stress response before it can slow down.

I personally learned that movement could be a more effective antidote for severe anxiety when I experienced my own panic attack several years ago. I awoke suddenly at 3 a.m. breathless, sweating profusely, with my heart racing at about 115 beats per minute. Being a therapist, I understood what was happening and initially responded by slowing my breathing, redirecting my thoughts, and attempting a few rounds of progressive muscle relaxation. To my dismay, these interventions didn't decelerate the rush of adrenaline coursing through my veins one bit.

Fortunately, I recalled a story from psychiatrist David Burns's book *Feeling Good* (1980) in which he suggested that one of his patients do jumping jacks as a way to distinguish a panic attack from a heart attack. Burns told the man that if he could do just one jumping jack, he could be fairly certain he wasn't having a heart attack. So I got out of bed and started doing jumping jacks. Surprisingly, I felt better within minutes. It wasn't so much that exercising allayed my fears of having a heart attack, but the cardiovascular activity itself provided relief. Exercising my body was matching what my nervous system wanted: to move, to run, to do something!

Because I'm not too fond of jumping jacks, I decided to continue exercising to an aerobic dance DVD. Within 10 minutes, my heart rate felt normal and I was able to finish with a few stretching and deep breathing exercises. Since having this experience, I often recommend clients try 10 minutes of brisk walking to reduce intense anxiety and quiet panic symptoms. My clients have agreed that incorporating several minutes of light physical activity is more effective than using breathing or relaxation techniques alone.

Research by psychology professor Robert Thayer bears this out. In Thayer's book *Calm Energy* (2001) he talks about an experiment he conducted in which he measured the subjective energy and tension levels of research participants after they walked briskly for 10 minutes. Results showed that participants reported a significant decrease in tension and an increase in energy level for up to 60 minutes after a 10-minute walk. Thayer explains that tension is caused when we inhibit the action tendencies our bodies want to take when stressed. Moving the body releases and tempers the emotional response the brain is urging the person to take.

Likewise, in her book, *8 Keys to Safe Trauma Recovery* (2010), Babette Rothschild recommends engaging in light physical movement to discharge the fight-flight-or freeze response. Rothschild reports moderate physical activity also regulates stress hormones and increases feelings of containment, strength, and self-control. To note, both Thayer and Rothschild state that prolonged, intense physical exercise is contraindicated for people dealing with depression, posttraumatic stress, and anxiety. Not only can extended exercise increase pain and fatigue but some people are also prone to panic or flashbacks when their heart rate increases dramatically because the body associates this with the fight-or-flight response. Therefore, it is better to start with lower intensity activities like walking, strength training, yoga, Tai Chi, or Qi Gong.

MINDFUL BREATHING AND MOVEMENT

Mindful movement activities not only assist clients in discharging stagnant energy, but they can also assist clients in staying present. I once worked with a client who could not stop pacing at night and did not know why he was doing it. He sat on my couch, bouncing his legs up and down, and asked if there was any way I could "knock him out" with hypnosis so he could sleep at night. Remembering Milton Erickson's philosophy of utilizing behaviors the client is already doing, I suggested he could actually go into a trance by pacing mindfully. I got up and paced back and forth with him, then coached him to gradually slow the pace and observe the feelings within his body as he took each step. He soon realized that his pacing symbolized his desire to "walk away" from an abusive relationship. For years, he'd learned to override his frustration by focusing on work, but the situation had become untenable and he realized that subconsciously, his mind was urging him to take an action.

Mindfully walking back and forth in my office also served as a way for this client to remain emotionally present when we reprocessed emotional memories with the RECON process. There are a number of ways you can use movement to assist clients in maintaining emotional presence such as throwing a beach ball back and forth, mirroring your hand movements, or even playing handclapping games with you. Focusing on this didactic rhythmic movement brings the client into connection with you and the present moment. In addition, doing these movements while simultaneously recounting an emotional memory can create a mismatch experience that triggers reconsolidation. Of course, bilateral stimulation moves that are used in EMDR can be useful for this purpose, too. For example, alternately tapping one's right and left leg at a pace of 60 beats per minute can assist the client in retrieving and reprocessing an emotional memory (Shapiro, 2001).

In sum, incorporating movement into your sessions is another way you can experientially alter a client's self-concept, reprocess traumatic memories, discharge anxiety, and shift mood. The simplest way to use movement is to bring the client's awareness to the way shifting body postures can alter his self-image and mood. Assisting the client in completing a survival response and acting out gestures that reflect a sense of triumph and mastery can reconsolidate traumatic memories. Clients may also find dancing to a music playlist helps them express and reprocess feelings related to significant events in their lives. Last, inviting keyed-up clients to take a take a 10-minute walk with you or leading them in slow, meditative movements can calm a restless, emotional brain. Of course, some of the somatically focused psychotherapy approaches I referenced in this chapter are more comprehensive than can be detailed in this book, and I encourage you to delve deeper into studying any of these models if they interest you.

My intention with this chapter, as with all the chapters of this book, has been to provide you with tangible techniques you could use right away with clients who were not responding to traditional approaches. In the final chapter of the book, I'll present how to bring all these ideas together as you form your own unique therapy style.

CHAPTER 11

Putting It All Together

Neuroscience is now validating what we've intuitively known as therapists: Problematic patterns are driven by the emotional brain, which learns through a *compelling, felt experience*, not logic-driven conversation. This principle is especially relevant for clients who rationally understand their issues, yet still feel unable to change. In this book, I've presented a number of ways you can create those felt experiences to change implicit patterns at deeper emotional levels and get your clients unstuck. But how do you put it all together? This chapter will take you through a case from start to finish, reviewing and illustrating how you can implement techniques from each chapter.

ENLIVENING THE THERAPEUTIC ALLIANCE

First, you enliven your therapeutic alliance by engaging your own emotional brain. Tune into the client's nonverbal cues, attending to the implicit conversation transpiring from right brain to right brain. Recognize the signs of attunement and misattunement so you can track, pace, and maintain a responsive connection. To transition from empathically pacing with your client to leading him toward change, use the "Align, Lift, and Lead" language pattern. You *align* with the client by using the "has been" tense change as you reflect your understanding of the problem. You *lift* the client by affirming his strengths, intelligence, and motivation. Here is how I used this language pattern in the first session with Emily, a 28-year-old client who had social anxiety:

"Emily, I understand that you have not been feeling comfortable talking to people you don't know that well. So I'm glad you're here. You're obviously motivated because here you are having a pleasant conversation with me, even though we don't know each other that well. So I'm seeing us expanding on skills you already have."

ELICITING EXCITING GOALS

Next, you want to elicit an exciting, heartfelt goal for your client that is intrinsically motivating. Lifeless, dry objectives such as "Client will talk to two new people per week" or "Client will reduce social anxiety by 50%" may please managed care providers, but they are not going to inspire your client. You have to look and listen for the people, goals, or activities that have real value and meaning for her. Look for the nonverbal cues. Notice which topics broaden her affect, animate her body language, trigger her curiosity, or otherwise stir her emotionally. For instance, I want to know *who* specifically Emily wants to feel less anxious around. Who is so important to her that she is willing to spend her time and money on therapy? To determine this, I ask:

"Emily, I really want this experience to be worth your while and help you achieve something that is really meaningful to you. Is there a certain person or group of people you're interested in feeling more comfortable around?"

Emily replied, "Well, a group of my coworkers has been inviting me out to lunch, but I've been avoiding it because I feel socially awkward. I'm afraid they would think I was weird or boring, but I kind of do want to get to know them better."

Now we've got a clear, meaningful goal: preparing Emily to feel more comfortable having lunch and socializing with her coworkers. To positively connect the emotional brain to a goal, anchor it to a multisensory image that represents the desired response. Begin by imagining the ideal way that you sense your client would like to be feeling, thinking, or acting. Then, share your vision with her and invite her to elaborate on it until you arrive at an image that seems agreeable. Here's an example of how I did this with Emily:

> *"Emily, let's create an image of the way you'd like your mind to be responding because the deeper mind connects better to multisensory images than it does to words. As I describe what I'm intending for you, envision it with me and let me know if it resonates with you. My intention is to have you feeling clear, secure, at ease, observing people with mild curiosity, demonstrating an interest in learning more about them whether you actually talk to them or not. I'm seeing you gaining full awareness that even if someone did make a judgment about you, you're learning something about him or her, not you. They are not the experts on you. You are the expert on you. Would it be okay to be thinking, feeling, and acting more like that? Or is there anything you would change? Emily replies, "I'd like to feel like that. But right now it doesn't seem possible."*

LOCATING THE ROOT OF AN EMOTIONAL CONFLICT

Like I experienced with Emily, if your client says the image doesn't seem possible or feel okay, then invite her to add or change any qualities she'd like. Many times when the image does not feel okay, it's either because the client doesn't think it is attainable or there is an emotional conflict about changing the pattern. Sometimes the client is conscious of the conflict, but many times she is not. In this case, explore any emotional memories where the original pattern was learned and reinforced.

In Chapter 4, I discussed how to locate emotional memories that maintain implicit patterns. Most of the time the client has not changed the pattern because it served an adaptive purpose at one time in his or her life. You can use the worksheet for Locating Embodied Beliefs that I've provided in Chapter 4 (Worksheet 4.1). You begin by asking the client to follow the sensations associated with the current undesired response back to an earlier time when he or she can remember having similar feelings. Following the sensations usually leads to a more relevant memory because emotional memories are stored more as felt encounters than explicit verbal accounts. Once your client has located a relevant memory, explore the implicit beliefs and action tendencies that got associated with it. Reassure the client that even if it doesn't make logical sense, the response was adaptive then, which is why the emotional brain hasn't changed it.

Whenever Emily thought about having lunch with her coworkers, she felt a pit in the bottom of her stomach. She traced this sensation back to a memory in middle school when a group of kids bullied her in the cafeteria at lunchtime. Emily coped by avoiding the cafeteria and catching up on her homework in the library. As a result, her parents and teachers praised her studiousness and good grades. Now, Emily avoids lunch with peers, opting to sit at her desk catching up on work, and gets praised by her boss for being so dedicated. But she feels lonely and miserable. Once Emily made this connection, she understood her mind had continued the pattern of working at her desk during lunch and avoiding her peers because it had been adaptive when she was younger.

To get the emotional brain to change a response that was once adaptive, you have to update it through a new experience that invalidates prior learning. However, according to new research on memory reconsolidation, we now know that you have to present the new experience in a particular way within a specific window of time for it to change.

REVERSING TRAUMA WITH MEMORY RECONSOLIDATION

Fifteen years ago, scientists still thought that once you learned a fear, it was virtually indelible. Exposure techniques and extinction trials suppressed fear learning, but learned fears often resurfaced in response to environmental cues months later. Fortunately, neuroscience has verified that you can erase the emotional charge from a memory, but a few key events must take place for the memory to permanently change or "reconsolidate." Ecker et al. (2012) were the first therapists to translate this research into applications for psychotherapy. They surmised that first you must reactivate the memory. Second, you have to simultaneously pair a mismatch experience that produces a prediction error from what the brain expects from the pattern. Last, you have to repeat the new learning experientially within 5 hours after the memory has been recalled. Ecker et al. (2012) also opine that any psychotherapy model that effects deep and lasting change appears to be following this pattern.

To simplify things, I've boiled the reconsolidation process down to a five-step protocol that I call the RECON process. The RECON process follows the brain's requirements for reconsolidation while being basic and flexible enough for you to adapt to your own practice, training, and theoretical orientation. I've provided a RECON reference sheet in Chapter 5 (Worksheet 5.1) and list the steps here again for your review.

1. Recall the current undesired response briefly.
2. Explore for a similar emotional memory and the associated beliefs and behaviors that got associated with it.
3. Create a calm, positive experience that elicits the desired response.
4. Observationally describe the memory while remaining emotionally present.
5. Neutralize negative emotional meanings with contrasting positive experiences that update the original learning.

At this point, Emily and I have already completed Steps 1 and 2 of the RECON process. She has identified the memory from middle school and the implicit belief that her peers will bully her for no apparent reason, especially at lunchtime. The associated behavior is to avoid lunch with peers and stay at her desk doing work because this keeps her safe and leads to praise by authority figures.

Bringing this memory and the associated beliefs to conscious awareness reactivates the memory, but for the reconsolidation window to open, you have to create a mismatch experience that contradicts what the emotional brain expects from the pattern.

INVOKING INSPIRATIONAL IMAGERY

Invoking imagery is one of the easiest ways to begin crafting mismatch experiences. Additionally, before clients review traumatic material they need to have a way to feel in control and prevent their nervous systems from going into hyperarousal or hypoarousal. Using imagery to create a calming, positive experience in Step 3 of the RECON process accomplishes both of these goals. Although some therapy models suggest the client create imagery to represent a "safe place" prior to reviewing traumatic material, I like to create a calming, positive experience by deepening the client's connection to her ideal image. This signals to the emotional brain that there can be a new ending to her trauma story and elicits hope and optimism for the client.

For Step 3 of the RECON process I asked Emily to again *imagine feeling secure, clear, at ease, observing people with a friendly curiosity, an interest in learning about them, feeling comfortable just observing, making eye contact, or simply smiling. If any of these people act in a rude or disrespectful way, I suggested she realize she just learned something about them, not herself, adding, "You have freedom and power now that you didn't have as a kid, Emily. Now if someone doesn't treat you with respect, you can leave or sit near someone who treats you with kindness and consideration. Let's create a symbol to represent your mind working this way, something in nature or an animal in the wild, what is it?"*

With her eyes still closed, Emily smiled and said, "A cat. They just hang out and don't take anything personally."

To move the client deeper into a calming, positive experience with her symbol, I asked Emily to imagine the image of the cat as she took three, slow, deep breaths. You can also use the Breath-Symbol Induction Script I provided in Chapter 6 as a guide.

Once the client seems sufficiently calm and is connecting with the qualities represented by her ideal image and symbol, then you can move on to Step 4 of the RECON process. In this step, the client will observationally describe the troubling memory while remaining emotionally present. As the client is recounting the memory, you want to listen for distorted meanings and assist her in updating her story in a way that is more useful.

CONJURING UP COMPELLING STORIES

We are neurologically wired to organize our experiences into story. You can tell amusing, compelling stories that prompt the client to look at her situation differently. Or you can prompt the client to revise her story in a way that puts her in the role of a heroine, victor, or innocent bystander that survived a harrowing experience. Always let the client tell her story first so that you can get a full understanding of what happened and how she experienced it. However, as described in Step 4 of the RECON process, coach your client to tell the story from an observational point of view while remaining emotionally present to avoid over-stimulating the nervous system. Additionally, describing the event from a present moment perspective begins to create a mismatch experience that triggers memory reconsolidation because the client is recalling the story without all the emotional arousal.

The easiest way for the client to change the story is to finish it with a new ending. New endings provide a different context for the event, which yields new meanings and resolution. The new ending doesn't have to be dramatic; it just has to be a later moment in the client's life when she was out of danger, was in a better situation, or felt competent or empowered.

The first time she told me her story, Emily ended the story by saying she hid in the library and avoided her peers. When I prompted her to consider a new ending, she recalled that one of the boys who teased her actually asked her to the prom in high school. This led her to remember that other members of the clique who bullied her invited her to a few parties, too. But Emily opted not to hang out with them because they drank a lot and seemed pretty closed-minded. Emily laughed as she retold the story, juxtaposing her middle school experiences with her high school experiences around this group of people. She saw more clearly that this group of kids would do just about anything to "fit in" and was glad she didn't compromise her values to be accepted by them.

PRIMING WITH PLAY AND HUMOR

Chapter 8 discussed how to use play and humor to reduce anxiety, neutralize the negative meanings of past events, and reinforce new behaviors. Play and humor can be used at any point in your sessions with clients who seem receptive, but it is especially useful for creating mismatch experiences in Step 5 of the RECON process.

Emily and I decided to act out a role play to reduce her anxiety and build her confidence. I suggested Emily could play a woman with a snobby attitude, snubbing her at the lunch table while I played Emily's role. Emily started the role play by wrinkling her nose and saying, "Who invited you to have lunch with us, creep?"
I answered matter-of-factly, "Linda invited me."

Emily continued, "Well I hope you don't think I can be seen hanging out with you, especially while you're wearing those ugly black shoes. And you should really consider doing something different with your hair."

I smiled and replied, "Oh, what a shame. I fixed my hair this way just for you."

Emily laughed and we continued for a couple more minutes. Letting Emily play the character she feared reduced her anxiety because she realized how insecure a person would have to be to make such insensitive comments. Next we reversed roles. I began with silly, exaggerated insults, then gradually transitioned to more realistic scenarios Emily feared such as stilted, awkward conversation. As we worked through her feared scenes, we practiced various ways of keeping a conversation going until she felt more confident. In the next session, we explored how Emily could use music and movement to manage her anxiety before a social event.

ROUSING WITH RHYTHM, MUSIC, AND POETRY

In Chapter 9, I discussed how music can influence mood, alter neurochemistry, and entrain the brain to calmer, meditative states. One activity most clients enjoy is creating a playlist of tunes that elicit desired responses. When creating a playlist, it is good to start with songs that match the client's current mood and gradually move toward rhythms that evoke the frame of mind the client desires.

> *Emily started her playlist with songs that reflected feeling like a social reject such as "Creep" by Radiohead and "How Soon Is Now?" by The Smiths. Next, she chose the song "Middle" by Jimmy Eat World that had encouraging lyrics and a fast beat. Emily ended her playlist with "Canned Heat" by Jamiroquai, the song that Jon Heder danced to in the film* Napoleon Dynamite. *In the film, Napoleon had been considered a social misfit, but when he danced to this song on the school's stage, his classmates cheered him on. Holding this image of* Napoleon Dynamite *in her mind was both amusing and reassuring to Emily. She listened to these songs in the morning before work to discharge her anxiety and bring herself to an optimistic frame of mind.*

INTEGRATING MINDFUL MOVEMENT

In Chapter 10, we discussed various ways movement can be used to reprocess traumatic memories and engender desired states of mind. Dancing to her playlist helped Emily shake off anticipatory anxiety, but I also showed her how to adjust her posture to increase feelings of security and confidence. Recall that carrying oneself with an upright, slightly relaxed posture has been shown to increase feelings of power and poise. In addition, I suggested Emily could place her hand on her heart or her abdomen to signal comfort and compassion toward herself. She practiced these postures with meditative breathing a few minutes before she out went to lunch with her coworkers. Although she said she didn't talk much the first time she went out to lunch with them, she focused on listening and learning more about her coworkers as we'd rehearsed in our sessions. Over the next several weeks, Emily's anxiety dissipated and she told me that one of her coworkers was turning out to be one of the best friends she'd ever had. In fact, about a year later, he asked her to marry him.

UNITING THE PSYCHOTHERAPY PROFESSION

This is one of the most exciting times in the field of psychotherapy. Recent discoveries about the workings of the emotional brain and memory reconsolidation allow us to be more intentional and effective with our clients in a way we have never been before. Additionally, I believe these neuroscience discoveries have the potential to unite the psychotherapy profession in an unprecedented way. Neuroscience studies now suggest that Freud wasn't far off in his theories about unconscious learning, motives, and drives. But fortunately we've learned that the unconscious isn't completely hedonistic but is actually an adaptive, well-intentioned, emotional brain. Skinner and the behaviorists were right in stating that our behavior is shaped by associative learning. But we know we aren't automatons and can influence our behavior with our thoughts, as the cognitive theorists proposed. However, the key is to integrate the best of what all the various theories have to offer and use our interventions more strategically.

As cognitive therapy proposes, we can still use our rational minds to identify maladaptive beliefs and behaviors. But to eliminate problematic emotional responses at their roots, we have to follow the brain's rules for memory reconsolidation and update implicit learnings through compelling, felt experiences as psychodynamic and humanistic theories have proposed. Once these implicit patterns are addressed and reconsolidated, new learning can further be reinforced with subsequent experiences and cognitive-behavioral interventions. As Ecker et al. observed, "With clear knowledge of the brain's own rules for deleting emotional learnings through memory reconsolidation therapists no longer have to rely largely on speculative theory, intuition or luck for facilitating powerful, liberating shifts" (2012, p. 4).

In other words, we don't have to guess at how to create "Aha" moments for our clients anymore; there are clear rules for how to achieve them. Eventually, I think our profession will agree on this basic premise and the only way therapy models will differ is in the various techniques they use for creating felt, transformational experiences. I hope this book has given you new ideas for how you will create those experiences for your clients. Moreover, I wish you and your clients much success and many more transformational "Aha" moments.

"AHA!" BONUS MATERIALS

If you would like to get more worksheets, creative tools, and demonstrations of how to use the techniques discussed in this book, please visit my Web site at http://www.courtneyarmstrong.net. You can find additional materials under a heading marked "Free Stuff" and in the articles on my blog.

Furthermore, I have created a 6-week online course called *The Therapeutic Aha: 10 Strategies to Get Your Clients Unstuck* that goes along with this book. In the course, you'll get weekly demonstration videos and teleconferences to help you craft breakthroughs with stuck clients and create a practice you love. Readers of this book get a 10% discount off the course; when you register, just enter the coupon code: UNSTUCK.

References

Achterberg, J. (1986). *Imagery in healing.* Boston: New Science Library.

Aesop. (2002). *Aesop's fables.* [iBooks iPad version] Champaign, Ill: Project Gutenberg. Retrieved from iBooks]

Agren, T., Engman, J., Frick, A., Bjorkstrand, J., Larsson, E. M., Furmark, T., & Fredrikson, M. (2012). Disruption of reconsolidation erases a fear memory trace in the human amygdala. *Science, 337,* 1550–1552.

Alberini, C. (2013). *Memory reconsolidation.* London: Academic Press.

Alexander, F., & French, T. M. (1946). *Psychoanalytic therapy: Principles and application.* New York: Ronald Press.

Armstrong, C. A. (2011). *Transforming traumatic grief: Six steps to move from grief to peace.* Chattanooga, TN: Artemecia Press.

Arntz, A., Tiesema, M., & Kindt, M. (2007). Treatment of PTSD: A comparison of imaginal exposure with and without imagery rescripting. *Journal of Behavior Therapy and Experimental Psychiatry, 38,* 345–370.

Badenoch, B. (2008). *Being a brain-wise therapist: A practical guide to interpersonal biology.* New York: Norton.

Bandler, R., Grinder, J., & Andreas, S. (1979). *Frogs into princes: Neurolinguistic programming.* Boulder, CO: Real People Press.

Bandura, A. (1977). Self-efficacy: Toward a unifying theory of behavioral change. *Psychological Review, 84*(2), 191–215.

Beck, A. T. (1971). Cognitive patterns in dreams and daydreams. In J. H. Masserman (Ed.), *Dream dynamics: Science and psychoanalysis* (Vol. 19, pp. 2–7). New York: Gune and Stratton.

Berger, J. (2006). *Music for the soul: Composing life out of loss.* New York: Routledge.

Bertolo, H. (2005). Visual imagery without visual perception? *Psicológica, 26,* 173–188.

Brefczynski-Lewis, J. A., Lutz, A., Schaefer, H. S., Levinson, D. B., & Davidson, R. J. (2007). Neural correlates of attentional expertise in long-term meditation practitioners. *Proceedings of the National Academy of Sciences USA, 104*(27), 11483–11488.

Bruner, J. (1987). *Actual minds, possible worlds.* Cambridge, MA: Harvard University Press.

Bruscia, K. E., & Grocke, D. E. (Eds.). (2002). *Guided imagery and music: The Bonny Method and beyond*. Gilsum, NH: Barcelona Press.

Burns, D. D. (1980). *Feeling good: The new mood therapy*. New York: Avon Books.

Burns, G. (2001). *101 healing stories: Using metaphors in therapy*. New York: Wiley.

Campbell, J. (1973). *The hero with a thousand faces*. Princeton, NJ: Princeton University Press.

Capacchione, L. (1991). *Recovery of your inner child*. New York: Touchstone.

Carney, D. R., Cuddy, A. J. C., & Yap, A. J. (2010). Power posing: Brief nonverbal displays affect neuroendocrine levels and risk tolerance. *Psychological Science, 21*(10), 1363–1368.

Connelly, J. (2014). *Rapid resolution therapy level 1 manual*. Tampa, FL: Author.

Cron, L. (2012). *Wired for story*. New York: Ten Speed Press.

Cuddy, A. J.C., Wilmuth, C. A. & Carney, D. R. (2012) The benefit of power posing before a high-stakes social evaluation. *Harvard Business School* working paper, 13-027. Retrieved from http://nrs.harvard.edu/urn-3:HUL.InstRepos:9547823.

Cuddy, A. (2012, October 1). *Amy Cuddy: Your body language shapes who you are*. Retrieved October 2014, from https://www.youtube.com/watch?v=Ks-_Mh1QhMc.

Dadds, M. R., Bovbjerg, D. H., Redd, W. H., & Cutmore, T. R. H. (1997). Imagery in human classical conditioning. *Psychological Bulletin, 122*, 89–103.

Damasio, A. (2010). *Self comes to mind: Constructing the conscious brain*. New York: Pantheon Books.

Darwin, C. (1899). *The expression of the emotions in man and animals*. Champaign, Ill: Project Gutenberg. Retrieved October 1, 2014, from the Project Gutenberg Literary Archive Foundation: https://www.gutenberg.org/files/1227/1227-h/1227-h.htm.

Doherty, W. (2012). One brick at a time. *Psychotherapy Networker, 36*(5), 22–28.

Duvarci, S., Mamou, C. B., & Nader, K. (2006). Extinction is not a sufficient condition to prevent fear memories from undergoing reconsolidation in the basolateral amygdala. *European Journal of Neuroscience, 24*, 249–260.

Dweck, C. (2006). *Mindset: The new psychology of success*. New York: Ballantine.

Ecker, B., & Hulley, L. (2011). *Coherence therapy: Practice manual and training guide*. Oakland, CA: Coherence Psychology Institute.

Ecker, B., Ticic, R., & Hulley, L. (2012). *Unlocking the emotional brain: Eliminating symptoms at their roots using memory reconsolidation*. New York: Routledge.

Epstein, S. (2014). *Cognitive-experiential theory: An integrative theory of personality*. New York: Oxford University Press.

Evans, J. S. B. T. (2008). Dual-processes accounts of reasoning. *Annual Review of Psychology, 59*, 255–278.

Farah, M. J. (1988). Is visual imagery really visual? Overlooked evidence from neuropsychology. *Psychological Review, 95*(3), 307–317.

Foa, E. B., Steketee, G., Turner, R. M., & Fischer, S. C. (1980). Effects of imaginal exposure to feared disasters in obsessive-compulsive checkers. *Behavior Research and Therapy, 18*, 449–455.

Friedman, E. H. (1990). *Friedman's fables*. New York: Guilford Press.

Gazzaniga, M. S. (2002, March). The split brain revisited. *Scientific American*, pp. 27–31.

Gershman, S. J., Jones, C. E., Norman, K. A., Monfils, M. A., & Niv, Y. (2013). Gradual extinction prevents the return of fear: Implications for the discovery of state. *Frontiers in Behavioral Neuroscience, 7*, 164.

Gilbert, P. (2009). *The compassionate mind: A new approach to life's challenges*. London: Constable.

Goldstein, A. (1980). Thrills in response to music and other stimuli. *Physiological Psychology*, 8(1), 126–129..

Grigsby, J., & Stevens (2000). *Neurodynamics of personality*. New York: Guilford Press.

Hackmann, A. Bennett-Levy, J., & Holmes, E. A. (2011). *Oxford guide to imagery in cognitive therapy*. New York: Oxford University Press.

Hoffman, J. (1995). *Rhythmic medicine: Music with a purpose*. Leawood, KS: Jamillan Press.

Hölzel, B., Carmody, J., Vangel, M., Congleton, C., Yerramsetti, S., Gard, T., & Lazar, S. (2011). Mindfulness practice leads to increases in regional brain gray matter density. *Psychiatry Research: Neuroimaging, 191*(1), 36–43.

Hume, D. (2011). *A treatise of human nature*. [Kindle iPad version]. Retrieved from Amazon.com. (original work published 1738)

Huron, D., & Marguilis, E. (2010). Musical expectancy and thrills. In P. Juslin & J. Sloboda (Eds.), *Handbook of music and emotion: Theory, research, and applications*, (pp. 575–604). New York: Oxford University Press.

Iacoboni, M., Molnar-Szakacs, I., Gallese, V., Buccino, G., Mazziotta, J. C., & Rizzolatti, G. (2005). Grasping the intentions of others with one's own mirror neuron system. *PLoS Biology, 3*(3), e79.

James, W. T. (1932). A study of the expression of bodily posture. *Journal of General Psychology, 7*, 405-437.

Johnson, S. M. (2002). *Emotionally focused couple therapy with trauma survivors: Strengthening attachment bonds*. New York: Guilford Press.

Johnston, A. (2000). *Eating in the light of the moon*. Carlsbad, CA: Gürze Books.

Juslin, P. N., & Vastfjall, D. (2008). Emotional responses to music: The need to consider underlying mechanisms. *Behavioral and Brain Sciences, 31*, 559–621.

Kahneman, D. (2011). *Thinking, fast and slow*. New York: Farrar, Straus & Giroux.

Katz, L. S. (2005). *Holographic reprocessing: A cognitive-experiential psychotherapy for the treatment of trauma*. New York: Routledge.

Kawakami, A. I., Furukawa K., Katahira K., & Okanoya, K. (2013). Sad music induces pleasant emotion. *Frontiers in Psychology, 4*. doi: 10.3389/fpsyg.2013.00311.

Keren, G., & Schul, Y. (2009) Two is not always better than one: A critical evaluation of two-system theories. *Perspectives on Psychological Science*, 4(6), 533–550.

Kershaw, C. J., & Wade, J. W. (2012). *Brain change therapy: Clinical interventions for self-transformation*. New York: Norton.

Kosslyn, S. M. (2005). Mental images and the brain. *Cognitive Neuropsychology, 22*(3/4), 333–347.

Kounios, J. & Beeman, M. (2009). The aha! moment: The cognitive neuroscience of insight. *Current Directions in Psychological Science. 18*(4), 210-216.

Kreiman G., Koch C., & Fried, I. (2000). Imagery neurons in the human brain. *Nature, 408*, 357–361.

Kurtz, R. (1990). *Body-centered psychotherapy: The Hakomi method: The integrated use of mindfulness, nonviolence, and the body*. Mendocino, CA: LifeRhythm.

Lakoff, G., & Johnson, M. (2003). *Metaphors we live by*. Chicago: University of Chicago Press.

LeDoux, J. E. (1996). *The emotional brain: The mysterious underpinnings of emotional life*. New York: Simon & Schuster.

LeDoux, J. E. (2000). Emotion circuits in the brain. *Annual Review of Neuroscience, 23*, 155–184.

LeDoux, J. E. (2007). An emotional brain. [Recorded by The Amygdaloids]. On *Heavy Mental* [mp3 file]. New York: The Amygdaloids (2008).

Levine, P. (1997). *Waking the tiger: Healing trauma: The innate capacity to transform overwhelming experiences*. Berkeley, CA.: North Atlantic Books.

Levitin, D. (2010). Why music moves us. *Nature, 464*, 834-835.

Levitin, D. (2006). *This is your brain on music: The science of a human obsession*. New York: Dutton.

MacLean, P. (1990). *The triune brain in evolution: Role in paleocerebral functions*. New York: Plenum Press.

Martel, Y. (2003). *Life of Pi*. Orlando, FL: Harcourt.

Mazza, N. (2003). *Poetry therapy: Theory and practice*. New York: Routledge.

McKinney, C. H., Antoni, M. H., Kumar, M., Tims, F. C., & McCabe, P. M. (1997). Effects of guided imagery and music (GIM) therapy on mood and cortisol in healthy adults. *Health Psychology, 16*(4), 390–400.

Mehrabian, A. (1971). *Silent messages*. Belmont, CA: Wadsworth.

Mehrabian, A. (2007). *Nonverbal communication*. New Brunswick, NJ: Aldine-Atherton.

Menon, V., & Levitin, D. J. (2005). The rewards of music listening: Response and physiological connectivity of the mesolimbic system. *NeuroImage, 28*, 175–184.

Miller, W. R., & Rollnick, S. (2002). *Motivational interviewing: Preparing people for change* (2nd ed.). New York: Guilford Press.

Mitchell, C. W. (2007). *Effective techniques for dealing with highly resistant clients* (2nd ed.). Johnson City, TN: Author.

Monfils, M. H., Cowansage, K. K., Klann, E., & LeDoux, J. E. (2009). Extinction reconsolidation boundaries: Key to persistent attenuation of fear memories. *Science, 324*, 951–955.

Nader, K. (2012, May 25). *Karim Nader: Memory manipulation*. Retrieved October 2014, from https://www.youtube.com/watch?v=Dan68pTqpxQ

Nader, K., Schafe, G., & LeDoux, J. (2000). Fear memories require protein synthesis in the amygdala for reconsolidation after retrieval. *Nature*, 406, 722–726.

Naparstek, B. (2004). *Invisible heroes: Survivors of trauma and how they heal*. New York: Bantam.

Neimeyer, R. A. (2012). Virtual dream stories. In R. Neimeyer (Ed.), *Techniques of grief therapy: Creative practices for counseling the bereaved* (pp.187–189). New York: Routledge.

Nissen-Lie, H., Monsen, J., & Rønnestad, M. (2010). Therapist predictors of early patient-rated working alliance: A multilevel approach. *Psychotherapy Research, 20*(6), 627–646.

Norcross, J. C. (2010). The therapeutic relationship. In M. A. Hubble, B. L. Duncan, S. D. Miller, & B. E. Wampold (Eds.), *The heart and soul of change: Delivering what works in therapy* [2nd ed., Kindle iPad version, Chapter 4.] Retrieved from Amazon.com.

Ogden, P., & Minton, K. (2006). *Trauma and the body: A sensorimotor approach to psychotherapy*. New York: Norton.

O'Hanlon, W. (2011). *Quick steps to resolving trauma*. New York: Norton.

O'Hanlon, W., & Beadle, S. (1997). *Guide to possibility land: Fifty-one methods for doing brief, respectful therapy*. New York: Norton

Oritz, J. (1997). *The Tao of music: Sound psychology – using music to change your life*. San Francisco: Red Wheel/Weiser.

Oyarzun, J. P., Lopez-Barroso, D., Fuentemilla, L., Cucurell, D., Pedraza, C., Rodriguez-Fornells, A., & de Diego-Balaguer, R. (2012). Updating fearful memories with extinction training during reconsolidation: A human study using auditory aversive stimuli. *PLoS One, 7*, e38849.

Panksepp, J., & Biven, L. (2012). *The archaeology of mind: Neuroevolutionary origins of human emotions*. New York: Norton.

Panksepp, J. (2009). Brain emotional systems and qualities of mental life: From animal models of affect to implications for psychotherapeutics. In D. Fosha, D. Siegel, & M. Solomon (Eds.), *The healing power of emotion: Affective neuroscience, development, and clinical practice* (pp. 1-26). New York: Norton.

Panksepp, J. and Burgdorf, J. (2003). "Laughing" rats and the evolutionary antecedents of human joy? *Physiology & Behavior 79*(3): 533-547.

Pascal, B. (1958). *Pensées* (T. S. Eliot, Trans.). New York: Dutton.

Pedreira, M. E., Pérez-Cuesta, L. M., & Maldonado, H. (2004). Mismatch between what is expected and what actually occurs triggers memory reconsolidation or extinction. *Learning and Memory, 11*(5), 579–585.

Pennebaker, J. W., & Evans, J. F. (2014). *Expressive writing: Words that heal* [Kindle iPad version]. Retrieved from Amazon.com.

Perls, F. S., & Miller, M. V. (2013). *Gestalt therapy verbatim*. Gouldsboro, ME: Gestalt Journal Press.

Pessoa, L. (2013). *The cognitive-emotional brain: From interactions to integration*. Cambridge, MA: MIT Press.

Pink, D. H. (2009). *Drive: The surprising truth about what motivates us*. New York: Riverhead Books.

Pinkola-Estes, C. (1995). *Women who run with the wolves*. New York: Ballantine Books.

Plato. (2005). *Phaedrus* (C. Rowe, Trans.). New York: Penguin.

Redondo, R. L., Kim, J., Arons, A. L., Ramirez, S., Liu, X., & Tonegawa, S. (2014). Bidirectional switch of the valence associated with a hippocampal contextual memory engram. *Nature Online*. doi: 10.1038/nature 13725.

Rogers, C. R. (1957). The necessary and sufficient conditions of therapeutic personality change. *Journal of Consulting Psychology, 21*, 95–103.

Rossman, M. L. (2000). *Guided imagery for self-healing*. Tiburon, CA: H. J. Kramer.

Rothschild, B. (2010). *8 keys to safe trauma recovery: Take charge strategies for reclaiming your life*. New York: Norton.

Sacks, O. (2007). *Musicophilia: Tales of music and the brain*. New York: Knopf.

Sapolsky, R. M. (1994). *Why zebras don't get ulcers: A guide to stress, stress related diseases, and coping*. New York: Freeman.

Schiller, D., Monfils, M., Raio, C. M., Johnson, D. C., Ledoux, J. E., & Phelps, E. A. (2010). Preventing the return of fear in humans using reconsolidation update mechanisms. *Nature, 463*, 49–54.

Schore, A. N. (2012). *The science of the art of psychotherapy*. New York: Norton.

Schwabe, L., Nader, K., & Pruessner, J. C. (2014). Reconsolidation of human memory: Brain mechanisms and clinical relevance. *Biological Psychiatry, 76*, 274–280.

Schwarz, R. (2002). *Tools for transforming trauma*. New York: Routledge.

Sevenster, D., Beckers, T., & Kindt, M. (2012). Retrieval per se is not sufficient to trigger reconsolidation of human fear memory. *Neurobiology of Learning and Memory, 97*, 338–345.

Shapiro, F. (2001). *Eye movement desensitization and reprocessing: Basic principles, protocols, and procedures* (2nd ed.). New York: Guilford Press.

Sharpless, B., & Barber, J. (2012). Corrective emotional experiences from a psychodynamic perspective. In L. Castonguay & C. Hill (Eds.), *Transformation in psychotherapy: Corrective experiences across cognitive behavioral, humanistic, and psychodynamic approaches* (pp. 31–49). Washington, DC: American Psychological Association.

Sheikh, A. (Ed.). (2002). *Healing images: The role of imagination in health*. New York: Baywood.

Siegel, D. (2010a). *The mindful therapist: A clinician's guide to mindsight and neural integration*. New York: Norton.

Siegel, D. J. (2010b). *Mindsight: The new science of personal transformation*. New York: Bantam Books.

Stone, R. (1996). The healing art of storytelling. New York: Hyperion.

Strack, F., & Deutsch, R. (2004). Reflective and impulsive determinants of social behavior. *Personality and Social Psychology Review, 8*, 220–247.

Strack, F., Martin, L. L., & Stepper, S. (1988). Inhibiting and facilitating conditions of the human smile: A nonobtrusive test of the facial feedback hypothesis. *Journal of Personality and Social Psychology, 54*(5), 768–777.

Subramaniam, K., Kounios, J., Parrish, T. B., & Jung-Beeman, M. (2009). A brain mechanism for facilitation of insight by positive affect. *Journal of Cognitive Neuroscience, 21*, 415–432.

Suzuki, A., Josselyn, S. A., Frankland, P. A., Masushige, S., Silva, A. J., & Kida, S.(2004). Memory reconsolidation and extinction have distinct temporal and biochemical signatures. *Journal of Neuroscience, 24*(20), 4787–4795.

Tafell, R. (2012). In search of the unspoken self. *Psychotherapy Networker, 36*(5), 30–37.

Thayer, R. E. (2001). *Calm energy: How people can regulate mood with food and exercise*. New York: Oxford University Press.

van der Kolk, B. A. (2006). Clinical implications of neuroscience research in PTSD. *Annals of the New York Academy of Sciences, 1071*, 277–293.

Watkins, J. G. (1971). The affect bridge: A hypnoanalytic technique. *International Journal of Clinical and Experimental Hypnosis, 1*, 21–27.

Watkins, S. G. (1992). *The practice of clinical hypnosis, Vol. 2. Hypnoanalytic techniques.* New York: Irvington.

White, M., & Epston, D. (1990). *Narrative means to therapeutic ends.* New York: Norton.

Willis, J. (2006). *Research based strategies to ignite student learning: Insights from a neurologist and classroom teacher.* Alexandria, VA: Association for Supervision and Curriculum Development.

Zaltman, G. (2003). *How customers think: Essential insights into the mind of the market.* Cambridge, MA: Harvard Business School Press.

Index

Note: Italicized page locators refer to figures.